# WISDOM

25 Solutions To Maximize
Fundraising Results

## MEAGHAN K. FOLEY

Printed in United States of America

First printing 2017

ISBN: 978-1-7341044-2-4

Published by BrightDot LLC
7424 Chapel Hill Rd, Suite 107
Raleigh, NC 27607
www.thebrightdot.com

# Foreword

*"The Future has several names: For the weak it is impossible; for the fainthearted it is unknown; for the thoughtful and vigilant it is ideal; The challenge is urgent; the task is large; The time is now!"*

— **VICTOR HUGO**

*FEAR* IS A FORBIDDING TERM.

*Anxiety* is for many of us, a scary reality.

Both are prevalent whenever one heads into an unknown sea. Both of these grip our world at this precise moment. It's not the first time.

I shall never forget my sixth-grade year in Winston-Salem, N.C. It was 1962. Russian missiles, 90 miles away from Florida, were aimed at us.

With a large GE facility in our town, a newspaper suggested we were in the top ten targeted towns to be bombed. Daily drills at Moore Elementary to protect us, had us going into the hall and ducking our heads between our knees.

My classmates' parents-built bomb shelters in their backyards. Nightly newscasts reported the sparring between the US and Russia. Fear and Anxiety ruled the day.

The death of John F. Kennedy followed several years later by the assassinations of Robert Kennedy and Martin Luther King, Jr., perpetuated an ongoing environment of unease that could have brought our country to its knees.

Since 2001, I have felt those same emotions bubbling up in the lives of co-workers, friends, and families. Terrorism, finances, insurance, and many other realities are strangling so many of our resolves to dream big about our jobs, our families, and our future.

David Wyeth in his book, *Crossing the Unknown Sea,* writes about his friend Joel, who learned that to be effective, he had to take an inventory of his own fears. "He did not," writes Wyeth, "have to overcome his fears. He simply had to know what he was afraid of… what stops us from speaking out and claiming the life we want for ourselves."

Gaining this *vertical intelligence* is a long journey.

It starts with the first step. This book offers 25 steppingstones to help you *shift* away from fear and anxiety by becoming more aware and disciplined.

The author is Meg Foley, a trainer and coach of professionals at Google and U.S. Military personnel, Meg not only offers us insights but give us practical tools to help us step forward into the unknown!

Meg is a remarkable, wise individual who has impacted my life in a tremendous way. I am excited about the transformational insights she offers here and the role she now plays as a member of the BrightDot team.

Regards,

Bill Crouch
CEO
BrightDot

# Introduction

What is Wisdom? According to Merriam-Webster's dictionary, wisdom is defined as knowledge (both philosophical and scientific), insight (ability to discern inner qualities and relationships), and judgment (good sense). How do you get wisdom, and when do you know you have it, may be the more challenging questions to answer?

I think we can agree that wisdom is not something you achieve and then you are done, nor is it something that you just wake up one morning to realize you now have. I also think that gaining wisdom is a continuous process and is not time or age based.

The culmination of awareness you choose to bring to the moment, and the micro-efforts you choose to take create ripple effects throughout your life. And, by maximizing every micro-effort, you create an opportunity to build effective habits and processes that connect you to your purpose, your bliss.

The premise of this book, therefore, is that you (anyone) can seek and create wisdom in any moment through awareness and micro-efforts, and that the payoff is huge. The purpose of this book is to guide and challenge you on how to choose awareness, how to build your repertoire of micro-efforts, and how and why to maximize those efforts.

The theme of this book is wisdom, not the philosophy of wisdom, but rather the practice of wisdom. Within the theme are five fundamental components. Why five? Well, there are many layered reasons for that number just as there are many layered reasons for each of the fundamental components. Let's start with the number five. Both our inner and outer worlds are layered with sets of five that create balance. We have the five senses, five digits on each hand and foot, five extremities (includes head).

We have the five elements that include earth, air, fire, water, and quintessence (the 5th element also known as spirit or heart), which is the glue of them all. In numerology, five represents harmony, balance, life path and compatibility. In the bible, five represents goodness and favor and when multiplied by itself (5x5) it represents grace upon grace. In radio communication, "five by five" indicates perfect signal strength or clarity. The number five resonates in many layered ways, and it will emerge frequently in this book because the five layers enhance the creation of wisdom.

So, here they are, the five fundamental components of wisdom: The first component is connection. Connection in this case implies that you are who you are in relation to others. Next comes adaptability, which is the ability to successfully interact in a variety of environments with a variety of people. The third component is to learn. To be aware entails a curiosity and openness to learn and apply new things. The fourth component is balance. When practicing balance, you learn how to shift both mentally and physically, without losing your equilibrium. Finally, the fifth component is purpose. Purpose creates an internal beacon that guides your thoughts and actions and aligns you with your end state.

How do I know that these are the five components? Because: For as long as I can remember (age 3) I've been acutely aware of and attuned to the smallest intricacies in human nature and relationships. I observe and I notice myself and others and our interactions and I analyze them from up close and far away.

I have a unique, almost preternatural ability to understand the human condition. I have an intense desire to participate in life and to present my discoveries for critical and fun debates. Plus, I'm charismatic and funny, so people relate to me. And I learn from them and enjoy them, which makes them want to tell me even more things about what it is to be human. And I read a lot across many genres (except scary ones, I get nightmares). Oh, and I guess I should mention that I have an advanced degree in psychology and have been studying the idea of wisdom for many years.

Now, enough about me, let's get back to you and the book. You may be inclined to, or maybe have been told to think BIG, create a BIG plan, and take BIG action when it comes to acquiring wisdom. Just the very word wisdom has a BIGness or vastness to it with a far-reaching or long-term connotation that deserves BIG attention. Well, I am taking you in the opposite direction towards wisdom: to think small, to create a small plan, and take small action when it comes to acquiring wisdom.

My rationale is in part because wisdom is elusive. In one moment, you have it, and in the next, it could be gone. Another reason is that wisdom is not a "thing" to be achieved, it's a state of being. This state is activated through thoughts, choices, and actions. It is practiced by recognizing and seizing every small opportunity in every small moment. Each one, in a given moment is in line with that state or it is not. Each one is small and not even measurable as a fragment of time.

There is a lot of science and purpose behind my suggested courses of action in this book, which I will explain in each chapter. In a nutshell, these small tasks are ideal ways to shape your brain and align yourself for success because they are 100% in your control. Also, because each of the tasks are small and easy to do, you are less likely to create resistance or barriers, which increases the likelihood that you will complete them and internalize their effects.

One caveat: even though the tasks are easy they do require consistency to build and groom a path of wisdom. However, the more you do them the less effort they will require. And the more you operate from a wisdom state of being, the easier and more effortless that state becomes. Soon you will automatically think and act from a state of wisdom without conscious effort. In essence, you will train yourself to be at ease in a state of wisdom and will find it more effortful to disconnect from this state than to maintain this state.

Enjoy!

Meg

# Contents

# Connection

*"We are who we are in relation to others."*

–DR. KATHARINE LESLIE

ONE OF THE BEST WAYS to learn about ourselves is by connecting with others. Connecting with others is an integral aspect of our development throughout the lifespan, which starts in utero. Connecting with others provides our developing brains and bodies with the much-needed feedback necessary to stimulate the mental, emotional, chemical, and physical pathways that allow us to grow, interact and survive.

Therefore, connecting to others is not just integral to our development, it's integral to our survival. Yes, it's true without connection, we would not survive. There may be that one extreme outlier you heard stories about who managed to survive as a hermit. However, even that person had connection to someone at some point during their development. Also, an outlier doesn't negate the vast body of research validating just how necessary connection is to our health, wealth, and well-being.

When you examine your connections with others you build self-awareness, which in turn leads to wisdom. There are a few different ways to exercise your ability to connect. I will give you five different ways to do this in the chapters ahead.

## THE WHO'S WHO

STEP ONE: KNOW PEOPLE. As the adage states, "It's not what you know, it's who you know." As you will discover in a later chapter, this adage is not entirely correct but does highlight the ever so important component of connection.

I am sure you have heard the term "circle of influence," and to put it simply, this is the circle or circles of people you surround yourself with. They are the people you interact with, attach to, identify with, and seek support from. They are vital to your well-being, your physical and mental health and even your livelihood. Most people assume their circle contains only those people they CHOOSE to be in their circle and ENJOY being around, such as friends and family (assuming you enjoy your family).

However, a circle of influence also contains co-workers, neighbors, and others you associate or interact with regardless of how much you enjoy them. Just to give you an idea, the average person has about 250 people in their circle of influence.

Imagine that all 250 people in your circle are influencing you...because they are, and not always for the better. Interestingly, research suggests that your circle can tell you a lot about your current and future life trajectory. For example, if you want to know your income potential, notice the average income of those you surround yourself with. That average is you.

If you want to know how fit and healthy you are, look at those you surround yourself with. If you want to know how attractive you are, notice your circle. If you want to know if you are a "good" person, check out your circle. Want to know your future? Your circle knows. Will you be married? How successful will your marriage be? Will you have kids? Will you have a successful career? Will you have a big house? Your circle is a pretty good indicator of who you are and where you are going.

If this seems uncomfortable to you, I get it. It is for me too. It's uncomfortable to consider my fate in the hands of those in my circle of influence, especially, when I look at who I am spending the most time with.  For example, my beautiful, rich, successful, happily married college roommate who I only interact with on Facebook a few times a year is in my circle of influence. Awesome!

However, so is my on-again-off-again friend who is always in and out of relationships, perpetually broke and complaining about one health issue after the next. And, because she lives in my town, I tend to see or talk with her every few weeks. Guess which friend has slightly more influence over my own life statistics? Yep, not the one I was rooting for. Which suggests I must make some changes. How about you?

The good news is that we have control over our own circle of influence. No, not control over the actual people, but control over whom we allow into our circle of influence.

Start with making a list of the people in your circle. This could take some time and may not be achieved in one sitting. However, this activity is a great tool for self-reflection and growing your wisdom. In addition, it will help you in creating a circle of influence that benefits your health, wealth and satisfaction.

Write on the list the names of those closest to you AND those you interact with most often. Keep in mind that these may not be the same. Consider my example of my two friends. My college roommate is one of my dearest and closest friends. She knows me better than almost anyone, yet I don't interact with her daily. So be clear and honest about those on your list.

Next, highlight those on your list that have the attributes, attitudes, lifestyle, emotions, etc. that you most want to emulate. Most likely, no one person will have ALL of them. My college roommate is a rare breed. You might highlight your single neighbor who works out every day, your sister who has the happiest kids, and your boss who has an amazingly successful career.  Start to notice what percentage of your circle has or lives in a way you identify with and contains the components you strive for. In addition, notice how often you interact with them.

You have just identified the people who can increase your chances of thriving. Consider if you can increase your chances even further by engaging with these people more often. Are there others like them you can add to your circle? How would you do this? When?

Let's flip to the other side of the equation and look at the anchors. Who on your list is not serving you? Who is weighing you down? Who is not reflective of the life you aspire to? More importantly, how often are you allowing yourself to interact with them?

This can be a touchy subject and may trigger your defenses. If this is the case for you, then dedicate your efforts to adding more inspiring people rather than weeding the garden. However, when you are ready, it's equally important to remove the anchors from your life as it is to bring in those people who lift you up. For one, having anchors in your circle may prevent you from drawing in the high caliber people you seek; they too may be seeking to increase their chances of thriving and therefore may not want to associate with someone who has a lot of anchors in their life. Secondly, people who hold you down are mentally, emotionally, and physically draining.

Okay, I have made it clear what your circle says about you and how to up your score card. I also should point out that this is not just about projecting or showcasing what you want to be based on your circle of influence. Like, "Hey, look at me. I have lots of rich friends, and I have Bill Gates on my speed dial." It's much deeper and more layered than just knowing people. It's about relationships. Specifically, relationships that exchange support, inspiration, and joy rather than drain energy, time and resources.

The very process of seeking out and maintaining these relationships forces you to build and reinforce those very attributes that make the relationships worth having. This includes gratitude, empathy, patience, compassion, love, confidence, etc. In essence, you receive what you give. By engaging in and maintaining healthy, happy relationships with healthy, happy people you both become even more so.

What's more, this creates a ripple effect of an ever-growing circle of more and higher caliber people. This is powerful!

**SMALL TASK:** *engage your list. Circle five people on your list that you highly value and have not reached out to in a while. Contact them today, check in and reconnect.*

## 2. JOY TO THE WORLD

NOW THAT YOU HAVE ASSESSED your oh-so-valuable circle of influence and understand you are only as strong as your circle, let's dive further into how to interact with your circle. Many of us interact through social media, which can be a great tool to stay in contact, but it doesn't foster deep connection.

For example, I might see on Facebook that my cousin Sara just had a baby. I find myself thinking "Oh wow, Cousin Sara just had a baby. How nice." Now I feel connected to her since I am informed about her situation. I also might reach out and say, "Congrats" on her Facebook page. (A half-hearted, even abbreviated congratulations with no substantial feeling or effort behind it). This might be enough to keep in contact but is it enough to develop the relationship?

I get it. Time is valuable. You only have so much every day and it doesn't roll over. This is one of the most common excuses I hear, and I even say it to myself occasionally when the question comes up, "Why don't you stay in touch?" I remind myself that people make time for the things that are most important. So, if I am not making time for this person then they must not be that important to me. When I hear it put this way, it gives me a jolt. First, I feel like a bit of a jerk because I realize, "You are not important" is the message I am sending to this person. Then, I commit to making it right.

To make it right and keep it right takes developing the right pattern of communication. Sporadic and infrequent surges into communication mode with long lost friends isn't it. I am not saying you should spend hours upon hours on phone calls catching up with each and every person you wrote on your list from the last chapter. I am saying that there are reasonable AND sustainable measures you can take to keep in touch with those you care about which don't require immense amounts of time.

For example, if Cousin Sara is someone I really care about and value in my circle and I see she just had a life changing event like having a baby, I can and should share in that with her by putting in more than a 1.5 second "Congrats" on her Facebook page. Can I call? Can I send a card? A gift? What can I do to share in this joy and cultivate our relationship?

Shelly Gable, a well-known researcher who specializes in connection, researched the key components to a successful relationship. She found that sharing in someone's good news is one of the most important ways to build strong relationships.

In addition to strengthening the relationship, sharing good news also multiplies feelings of joy in BOTH of you. Even if it's not your good news, reliving someone else's joyful thing, even briefly, ignites a joyful state in you. Pretty crazy, huh?

Imagine if you decided to go around all day and ask people, even strangers, to tell you about their good news; it would light you both up and you could essentially use their joy to make you more joyful ALL DAY. It's like a free and cordless battery charger that can jolt you and the person you're talking to into immediate feel-good mood!

How often do we access this wonderful joy button? Again, if you find yourself using that tired, "but I don't have time blah, blah, blah" consider the message I said earlier, "You are not important." Is that what you mean to say? I didn't think so.

This process does not have to be time consuming. In the same amount of time it takes to half-heartedly listen to your spouse or child tell you about their day while you check your work email, you could have been boosting both your joy states and strengthening your relationship. Instead, you tried faking your way through the conversation, felt no real shift in your own state and made no impact.

Actually, that is not true. You did make an impact and it's not the one you want to hear. The research shows that not sharing in someone's joy erodes the relationship. Let's unpack this a little more. If you are distracted, attempting to multitask, not making eye contact, etc., the other person can tell (even over the phone), and they don't like it. Think of it this way, can you tell when someone is doing this to you? I'm guessing that's a big yes, so the same is true the other way around. The message: DON'T BE THAT GUY/GAL!

What do you do instead? You look for moments to share in someone's joy as often as you can. Again, I said moments, not hours or days. You actually listen to what they are talking about and ask them to tell you more. You pick up on their enthusiasm and allow yourself to feel it too. Your goal is to have someone walk away feeling better than they felt when they approached you. If they walk away looking deflated, quiet, hunched, sunken, etc. you just eroded the relationship and need to regroup and try again, ASAP.

Rather than waiting for someone to come to you with good news, you can initiate someone's good news as well. Ask them to tell you something good that happened. No matter how big or small. Everyone can find something good that happened to them. Get them to tell you about something good and engage with them. Notice how you feel; notice how they feel. Notice if the connection increased. I have a good friend who says, "Tell me something good" instead of, "How's it going?" when he interacts with people. I love this because it invites a much different conversation.

If you do this often and deliberately you will create a new pattern of communication for yourself. You will not only feel better yourself, but those in your circle will also feel better, and your relationships with those people will be stronger. You may even cause a ripple effect that will impact the way those you communicate with interact with others in their circle (which includes you by the way). What you put out will come back to you. Wouldn't it be nice to get a special card or gift from Cousin Sara when you have a joyful moment?

---

**Small task:** *share joy today. Choose five people on your list to share joy with. Ask them to share with you something positive, big or small, that happened to them recently. Then expand their joy by asking questions so they can relive the experience and the feeling. Notice how they shift.*
*Notice how you feel as well.*

---

## 3. CALLING MOTHER TERESA

ACTIVELY GIVING IS ANOTHER ONE of the best ways to reinforce connections and maintain strong relationships. Just like with the sharing joy technique, giving to others gives *you* a boost of positive emotion. What's more, when you give, you ignite gratitude in the other person, which is one of the most powerful rejuvenation emotions one can experience. And let's not forget about the ripple effect giving creates when the person you gave to gives back to you, and/or pays it forward to others. In other words, giving is contagious.

Crouch and Associates, the organization who published this very book, was created on the premise of giving. Their mission is to serve those who serve others. This speaks to the ripple effect that giving creates. The concept of paying it forward is not only mathematically viable but extremely effective.

The science of giving has to do with the chemical response it ignites in us when we give. The act of giving drives the emotion of gratitude. Gratitude is powerful because of the un-doing effect it has on the negative consequences of stress. Gratitude triggers neurotransmitters and hormones that bring your mind and body into balance. As a result, the damage caused by the neurotransmitters and hormones released when we experience a stressful situation are mitigated. Similar un-doing occurs with other positive emotions. Research shows, however, that gratitude is one of the most powerful triggers.

More than just a smile and momentary bond, giving causes a whole ripple effect of emotions, chemicals and physiological shifts that improve our health and well-being; giving triggers the emotions that trigger the chemicals that heal our bodies and give us energy. It's a feel-good boost that triggers our body and mind to say, "Hey, give me some more of that!" Plus, these chemicals reinforce our desire to give again and more often, which creates a giving pathway in the brain.

Thus, by giving you are also receiving. This may sound self-serving, and it is. There is no such thing as "selfless" service AND that is perfectly ok. Receiving benefits keeps us giving more. If you doubt just how powerful these shifts are, next time you are having a down day, give to or do something heartfelt for someone else. More specifically, give someone a thank you. This is a small giving gesture with a big result. Notice the immediate shift in your body, mind and in the connection between you.

As with all the skills and techniques in this book, going through the motions does not work. When you do something mindlessly, you receive no benefit and get no closer to wisdom. For example, saying a quick and empty "thanks" via text is not exactly gratitude evoking and thus has little impact on either you or the person you are texting. On the other end, spending 10 minutes thanking the grocery clerk for helping you with your groceries is excessive. Again, I will go back to finding a balance and creating consistent processes.

Thank you's can and should be more than words and of course are not the only form of giving. However, developing a consistent thank you pathway for giving is highly advantageous both personally and professionally. A wonderful routine might be to send five thank you cards a week or thank-you gifts, notes, etc. to people in your circle of influence or people who have assisted you in some way. This process will shift your awareness to recognize more and more opportunities to give, to experience gratitude and to connect in a meaningful way.

---

SMALL TASK: *thank-you cards. This week send thank you gifts or cards to five people on your list. Notice how it feels to plan and/or write the thank you? Notice how you feel after you send it? Is that a feeling you would like to experience more often? Luckily you know an easy way to reignite it now.*

## 4. "PLEASE SIR, CAN I HAVE SOME MORE?" (OLIVER TWIST)

IF GIVING COMES NATURALLY TO YOU, meaning you already have a deeply grooved pathway for noticing and seizing opportunities to give to others, then receiving from others is the next skill to consider. In yoga, there are two hasta mudras called varada and Abhay Prada. These hand positions are energetic symbols for the balance between giving and receiving. It is understood that imbalance in these areas creates imbalance in the mind and body. Our ability to give and receive should be fluid and equal, which enhances our inner balance and opens us to wisdom.

To some, receiving is thought of as bad or selfish. Conversely, to some giving is thought of as selfless and thus a good thing. If this is your belief, as it once was mine, let me set the record straight. BOTH giving and receiving are self-serving AND good things. BOTH are also connection building. Yes, it's true, receiving from others, as in letting others give to you, is just as important in relationship building as giving to others.

I was notoriously a give person and not a receive person. Here's a great example of why this was problematic. My ex-boyfriend noticed the floor mats of my new car were in the trunk rather than inside the car where they should be. As a small giving gesture, he offered to put them in the car for me. Practically before he could finish his offer I ran outside and put them in the car myself because I didn't want to trouble him with a chore. Notice he is my ex, as in the relationship failed partly because I never gave him a chance to give. In my mind it would be a burden to *make* him do that for me. In his mind it would be a gift he could give to show he cares. Sadly, I have many, many stories of my inability to let others give to me. It took a long time to realize the value of receiving.

Whether this imbalance resonates with you, or you already are very comfortable with receiving, let's get to the science behind it. As in giving, the same feel-good emotions come into play when receiving. That is, if you allow them. For me, receiving from someone ignited negative feelings because I associated receiving as burdening the other person. I didn't consider that their giving to me was a benefit to them. Once I reframed my interpretation from a burden to a benefit my relationships became stronger and more intimate. My relationship world completely changed.

When you allow others to give to you, you benefit from that powerful emotion of gratitude, and they benefit from the powerful emotion of joy. Win-win! Together you have created one more layer of strength and connection between you. What a powerful tool! Let people help you! This includes times when you may not need it. For example, I don't need my five-year old nephew to help me with the dishes and it will likely take longer if I do. However, it's not about the dishes. He wants a chance to give, and it will provide us a chance to connect and grow our relationship. So now it becomes a no brainer question. Of course, I will let him help me with the dishes. Let's get a boost of happy together!

**SMALL TASK:** *let them help. Today when someone asks you if they can help you with something, let them. Or ask someone for help. Look for an opportunity to receive and let another give to you. Notice how you feel. Notice how they feel. Notice the connection.*

## 5. GOOD TALK

WORDS ARE WONDERFUL! And words are detrimental! The point is there are many ways to say any one thing, and some ways are more harmful than others. And it's not just the words you choose, it's also how you say those words (e.g., tone, pace, inflection). No wonder texting can get us into trouble. How often have you received a text, and you had no clue if the sender was angry or happy or somewhere in the middle? Have you ever guessed wrong? Yikes.

When it comes to communicating effectively, in many of the organizations and individuals I work with, texting and emails are the go-to methods of communicating, supposedly because they save time. However, I often see the time-consuming aftermath of rushing through our communications, such as an awkward and heated back and forth of more rushed and unclear words, texts and emails to clarify something that should've been said more effectively the first time.

My mind-blowing solution is not to use more words. It's to use less words, and most importantly to use THE MIGHTY PAUSE. A pause is the most time effective, relationship enhancing, even life-saving tool in your wisdom toolbox. It's quick and easy to do because you DO nothing. Well, nothing isn't accurate because you DO sit, breathe, and collect your thoughts. In this moment of pause and collection you sort through all the millions of words, emotions and reactions zooming through your head space, and then you craft your sentences with the words that carry the most clarity and understanding.

During the pause, you should also be analyzing the other person's words, emotions, and reactions. This is important for accuracy. You use this information to choose your words and craft your sentences to set yourself up for success. This simply means to get your message out in a way that will be accurately received.

When it comes to communication, I often say communication is the feedback you get. If I think I said something clearly and concisely and there is no possible way I could be misunderstood, yet the other person looks at me with a confused look or gives a defensive response, then I did not communicate effectively. It does not mean *they* are the problem. While they do have a role in the conversation, if I play the blame game or point the finger, I am not setting us up for an achievable outcome. And I am not seizing the situation to practice wisdom.

When you become mindful of how your message is being received it will significantly enhance your ability to adjust and speak in a way others will understand. The other piece is to listen to their message and be sure you are receiving it the way they intended. The key to good communication is to NEVER ASSUME. Simply ask.

Asking for clarity is another highly valuable and underutilized tool to communicate effectively. Just by incorporating the pause and the ask consistently in your interactions your relationships will dramatically improve! And you will save a lot of time. You can prevent that jumbled, conflict ridden and unnecessary round about game of, "What the heck are you saying to me?"

**Small task:** *exercise*

*THE MIGHTY PAUSE.*

*There are millions of words. Choose them wisely and practice the pause. Take those extra few seconds to craft the sentences that relay your intended meaning. Also, ask for clarity. Ask the other person if they understand and can tell you what you just said. Notice how this feels. Use both tools five times today.*

# Adaptability

*"It's not the strongest or most intelligent that will survive but those who can manage change."*

**- LEON C. MEGGINSON**

AT ITS MOST BASIC LEVEL, adaptability is about surviving in varying environments and situations. By actively practicing and becoming proficient at adapting, you can shift from a basic survival level into a thriving level. In this process of learning how to adapt in a variety of situations, environments and with other people, you are also gaining wisdom.

This process requires learning how to pause, notice, evaluate and engage in different situations and environments. These activities are not cut and dried, they are fluid and moving and vary based on the situation and environment. People who are highly adaptable can comfortably shift through these activities quickly and accurately. For these reasons, adaptability, like wisdom, is not something you achieve and then you are done. Adaptability requires continuous learning and effort.

The chapters in this section give you some strategies and tools to enhance your adaptability. The good news is once you implement these processes and make them habitual your ability to adapt will become more effortless. This will lead to enhanced wisdom.

## 6. EARLY BIRD GETS THE WORM

BEING PROACTIVE IN SEIZING opportunities is a great life skill. I don't mean opportunity in a BIG sense. I am referring to a moment in which a small micro-effort can provide an opportunity to practice being in a state of wisdom. The first step to being proactive in seizing opportunities is to notice.

Noticing requires being present, which entails intentional observing and analyzing. Seizing opportunities requires transforming intention and analysis into an action. Moving ideas to action creates neural pathways that trigger you to execute that transformation quicker and easier. Each time you trigger those pathways you increase the automaticity of this process. Eventually that pathway fires so quickly it feels effortless.

What does this have to do with the early bird? Well, the early bird seizes the opportunity to catch the worm by getting to it before any of the other birds. This metaphor highlights the importance of punctuality; the early bird wins because she got the worm. More so, she created a brain pathway for punctuality and at the same time she avoided the consequences of being late. We already talked about the benefit and detriment of first impressions in the previous section. This first impression is certainly one of the reasons punctuality is essential. However, the more important consequence is the effect being late has on your brain and your body.

If you ask anyone in the military, being early is ALWAYS synonymous with being on time and being on time means being late. The military knows why this is important. When we are in a rush it causes a surge of fight or flight hormones in our system. When we experience this surge a myriad of symptoms and effects occur. These may include increased heart rate, perspiration, shakiness, limited fine motor function, limited cognitive function, restricted emotional regulation, dry mouth and even bowel issues. This is our body's natural response to heightened activation in order to mobilize energy to our extremities that allow us to fight or flee. All this is triggered just by being in a rush.

Most people do not know how to effectively control and regulate fight or flight responses. As a result, they are forced to tolerate and suffer through these symptoms. This could mean showing up to an important meeting with pit stains, bowel issues, clammy palms, a foggy brain, and a feeling of anxiety. I don't know about you, but in my interactions with other people I would rather not have any of these symptoms.

Whether you are experienced at calming yourself down or not, the ultimate issue is that this causes one big energy leak. Even when experiencing a small level of the symptoms associated with being rushed, you are triggering the fight or flight activation. This means you are wasting energy, essentially leaking energy. You are burning up resources that you may need to get through your day. This may be how you survive but not how you thrive.

Let's consider the flip side. When you show up on time (or early) to your meeting, you are more likely to be in control of your thoughts and emotions, to think clearly, to communicate effectively and to maintain your energy. You have essentially maximized and regulated your energy. Not to mention, you don't have to hide pit stains all day.

Being punctual allows you to have a more successful interaction with the environment that you are showing up to; you have a few moments to get a lay of the land, observe the setting, and learn about the situation and the people you will be interacting with. And, you have established a first impression that benefits you.

Punctuality may seem like something only your dad would nag you about; however, by now you are probably looking at it differently. But don't think being punctual one time is enough, or that you will be punctual only when you have important meetings.

It is necessary to practice punctuality. If you are not practicing punctuality every day, then you are grooving an ineffective habit. If you are grooving the, "I'll be fashionably late" pathway 90% of the time, you have now groomed a superhighway of lateness and a body leaking fight or flight energy. Then when you attempt to be early or even on time it becomes very effortful and may not be possible at all.

Our habits are powerful tools that work for us or against us. When it comes to punctuality, be deliberate with the message you want to send. Recognize all the benefits of being early and feeling calm as well as the detriments of being late and feeling rushed. Then decide what is more in line with your path to wisdom. Choose the small moments to exercise this path so it will be automatic during the big moments.

**SMALL TASK:** *be punctual (early) today. Everywhere you go today plan to be there at least 15 minutes early. Is this easy or hard for you? What does it feel like to arrive early? What do you notice in your physiology? How will you maintain this every day?*

## 7. DRESS THE PART

WISE PEOPLE HAVE THE ABILITY to interact with diverse groups of people. They understand the etiquette and expectations of various and unfamiliar environments. And they typically dress appropriately to meet those expectations. I'm not implying that you must choose attire that is uncomfortable or radically different from your style. You should feel comfortable in what you wear and dressing in attire that represents you, even in a small way, helps you feel more comfortable. That being said, your attire ALWAYS says something about you, so choose wisely.

The first step to "dressing the part" is knowing the part. What do you know about where you are going and the people who will be there? Gathering information about the place and people you will be meeting with is a small effort that is easy and valuable. Keep in mind it's not just about how you interpret the environment; it's about anticipating how the environment will interpret you.

The next step is to decide what message you want to send and to what degree. For example, let's say I have an interview with the military. I might decide I want to send the message that I stand out from the group and that I have an edgy, fun, personality. Therefore, I decide to wear a bright red blouse and my favorite sparkly earrings with a black suit. I would not wear my bright red pants and low-cut sequined blouse that also show my edgy and fun personality. While both outfits send a stand-out message, the degree of that message is vastly different.

If you read this thinking a red shirt and sparkly earrings are not exactly representative of an "edgy" personality, then you did not pay attention to the first step. The military environment is conservative and highly perceptive of attire; it's a part of their culture. Knowing this, I must consider what message I want to send. I can dress in bland clothing just to fit in, but I would not feel comfortable, and I would not stand out. I can dress in clothing that makes me completely comfortable but may offend the interviewers, which would likely cause them to write me off. Or I can compromise and dress in a way that allows me to feel like myself *and* engage comfortably in the environment. Hence the red shirt, sparkly earrings, and black suit.

There are many underlying reasons it is beneficial to master this special blend of matching the environment while maintaining uniqueness - including a scientific reason.

We have a biological response in our brains to be leery or skeptical of those things, people and places that are vastly different from us. It comes down to a survival response in our programming. Let's take it back to caveman days. If the caveman stumbles into a new part of the forest and finds some beautiful flowers and a saber tooth tiger, which one is necessary for him to avoid in order to survive? It's far more beneficial to his survival to notice the danger in the environment than the pleasantries. We still respond this way. When confronted with something new or different, we tend to view it as potentially dangerous.

Again, this is a natural brain process. As evolved beings, we can override this instinct and choose not to let it impact us, but it is always there, and we are not always successful at blocking it. How does this relate to an interview? Well, first you should notice and keep in check your own survival response to new people and different environments. Secondly, be mindful of how and when you might trigger someone else's survival instinct. One way to avoid triggering their survival response is to dress the part.

The flipside of responding to new and different things and people with a danger response is to respond to that which is familiar and those that are most like us with trust. Again, some of us are far better and willing to allow this trusting response to lead, while others resist and block it.

When you meet someone for the first time who you hope to impress, would you prefer to trigger their gut reaction that says, "There's something about this guy/gal that I like" or "I'm not sure about this person." The reality is that you are triggering one or the other before a single word is exchanged. Don't leave it up to chance. Be deliberate in creating an atmosphere of trust. As I said earlier, your attire is ALWAYS sending a message, choose wisely...

---

**SMALL TASK:** *match and wear. Today deliberately plan your attire to incorporate elements that match your social environment. This will require some research as to who will be there and their social preferences. Add components to your attire that are comfortable and true to your style, but not overwhelming to the situation.*

## 8. PUT 'ER THERE PARTNER

ONCE YOU HAVE PUT YOUR FOOT in the door by dressing the part, you can open it further with a solid handshake. This might seem like a small and overly simple task, but again remember the focus of this book - small and easy. Wisdom is about focusing on simple and deliberate thoughts, choices and actions. A handshake is a valuable and informative aspect to an interaction with someone new.

Consider for a moment some of the hands you have shaken. Does it trigger an immediate impression when someone clamps down on your hand way too aggressively and tugs way too hard? How about the timid hand shaker who only gently grazes your fingers before pulling back and breaking contact?

Whether you realize it or not, you are constantly assessing your environment and all the people in it. Your brain has a judgment mechanism embedded in its wiring that causes you to make assessments and predictions on anything and everything in your space. This goes back to that survival response of being able to recognize danger. Our brains make an assessment, whether we like it or not. You are advanced enough to override initial impressions if you so choose. However, many people do not think beyond their initial impressions. Therefore, the saying, "First impressions are lasting impressions" rings true. When noticing a first impression we can choose to let it ride, which is the easiest brain pathway because it is already embedded as an innate structure. Or we can choose to lay a new pathway.

Many of us will stick with the first thought or impression we had, and not take the time to analyze further. That means your first impression is...impressionable. Others are making a snap judgment about you, just as you are making one about them. You are sending a message, so set yourself up for success by making deliberate, effective impressions.

If you are able to be shaking hands you have initiated connection. This means the person you are standing before is potentially one who could be in your circle of influence. This person also has a circle of influence whom they interact with often. Do you prefer them to be an advocate for you or a nay-sayer about you? More immediately, do you want them to tune in and listen intently to the things you are about to say or be disengaged? The answers to these questions will be dictated by the handshake, the first point of contact and entry point to connection.

No matter what level of importance you place on this specific interaction, this interaction, just like *every* interaction, is an opportunity to practice embracing a moment of wisdom or allowing it to pass you by. If you embrace this moment, you will see it as a valuable moment for experiencing the end state of being that you seek. How would the wise version of you shake this person's hand? What message are you sending in this hand-to-hand connection?

**SMALL TASK:** *shake some hands. Notice the impressions you get about others when you shake their hands. Do you let that impression guide you or do you override it? Assess the quality of your handshakes. What message does your handshake send? Practice shaking hands with people you already know and ask for feedback.*

## 9. ARE YOU PICKING UP WHAT I'M PUTTING DOWN?

THE LAST TWO CHAPTERS FOCUSED ON SKILLS that set you up for success prior to uttering a single word. Assuming you have done that, you can take the next step to mastering your social environment: speaking the language. I am not referring to learning a foreign language, although in some cases it may be necessary to learn a foreign language, but let's save that for the learning section. The idea of speaking the language is about understanding variations in communication.

Here's an example. The United States military is an environment with a very specific language. It's still English, but there are some very strong guidelines about how to address military personnel and what to address them with. In my usual or familiar environments, I might greet someone by saying, "What's up?" with a slight upwards head nod. This is a light and casual question that represents my light and casual nature. However, if I attempted to greet an Army General with "What's up?", I would have a

major issue with that General and with every other soldier and/or civilian within earshot.

Instead of sending the message that I am light and casual, I am sending the message that I am disrespectful and uneducated about the Army and do not belong in this environment. Those are strong messages (and not an exaggeration). While it may be possible to come back from that, do I really want to begin our interaction at a deficit? Had I done some homework and had even a small amount of understanding about the language of the military environment I could have initiated a much better start.

This is not just a point about etiquette. I want to make a connection. I could have stood there saying nothing and waited to be introduced, which may be good etiquette. However, I want to make a good impression and build connection, which requires speaking the language. Especially if I am working on enhancing my circle of influence.

This doesn't mean I need to know *everything* about the language of the environment. For instance, I may not need to know the exact rank on every soldier's jacket, but I do need to understand that I am entering a very formal setting where chain of command and respect are paramount. Knowing this, I may adjust my greeting by saying, "Hello Sir" accompanied by a proper handshake. This greeting will likely allow me to continue to engage with the General. My "What's up?" opening would have ended the conversation before it even started.

You must speak enough of the language to get your foot in the door. However, having more information is better than less. If I knew the General's rank and addressed him properly, I would send the message that I am respectful, and I have done my homework. He may even be impressed that I, a civilian, knew something about the military, even if it is just his rank.

I cannot emphasize enough how helpful it is to do some homework before entering a new environment. You are sending a message by what you wear or don't wear, and by what you say or don't say, so choose *wisely*. If you are not sure, ask. By asking someone more about their world you are showing interest and building connection and enhancing your adaptability.

To effectively speak the language takes awareness of the intricacies of that language. One of the best ways to expedite this effort is to use the common words or phrases spoken and understood by the person or group you are conversing with. When I am teaching effective communication to the sales department of a finance firm, I use their language. I will use terms like interacting with a lead, finding pain points, drawing out objections and closing the deal.

When I am teaching effective communication to the fundraising department of a nonprofit, I will use terms like engaging a potential donor, discovering their why, asking for a gift, and stewardship. I am teaching effective communication in both settings, but my language is very different because I understand the environments.

Speaking the language isn't just necessary in professional interactions. This process of speaking the language requires practicing in different environments and being consistent in your efforts. Consider how you chat with your kids. This may be especially noticeable if you have teenagers. How foreign is their language? How much easier would it be to interact if you knew a little more about their world? Even just a few facts about the latest pop culture, fads, acronyms, slang, and trends can go a long way.

This past Christmas my nephews asked me for presents related to Skylanders. I knew nothing about Skylanders. I took time to learn that this is not just a TV show or series of figurines but also a very elaborate and interesting video game. I informed myself enough to buy them both Skylander presents they would like and didn't already have. Then when I arrived for Christmas, I asked them to tell me more. I learned about the characters they love most, and even played the video game with them.

You might wonder what a video game has to do with wisdom, but you might be missing the point. It was never about the video game. I learned to speak their language. I also learned something new and discovered another way to connect with my circle of influence. I expanded myself; I practiced flexibility and adaptability in a previously unfamiliar environment.

> **SMALL TASK:** *speak a new language. Today, start a conversation with someone you often interact with. Learn about their world or an environment in which you don't feel comfortable. Practice interacting through speaking this new language. Notice how you feel and notice if your efforts enhance your ability to interact and build connection.*

## 10. MI CASA ES SU CASA

HOW WELL DO YOU HOST? I've placed quite a bit of emphasis on how to handle unfamiliar environments. The ability to adapt in unfamiliar settings is vital. However, so is the ability to welcome others into your environment. How well do you do this? Do you notice when someone feels uncomfortable? Do you try to help people feel comfortable in your environment? If so, how? If not, why?

It is not entirely your job to help another person feel comfortable. That person has some responsibility in the situation. However, you will benefit by taking the initiative in welcoming someone who enters your environment.

Here's a great example. A friend of mine works at a bio-tech firm. This firm often has outside organizations and investors coming to the office for various reasons. When she first started working at this company, she noticed something she considered to be very odd. From her cubicle, she noticed that when a guest came to the office no one greeted them. They were ignored until the person they came to see met them in the waiting area. No one said hello, or offered them water or, showed them where the restrooms were. She noticed these guests, some of them very vital to the firm's bottom line, looked very uncomfortable.

She decided to seize the opportunity. She started to quickly jump up and welcome visitors when they entered the waiting area. She simply thanked them for coming and offered them some water. She didn't do this to get ahead, she did it because it felt like the right thing to do. She acted from a place of wisdom. However, it was in seizing small and simple opportunities such as these that launched her career very rapidly.

My friend took it upon herself to welcome and engage with visitors, and as she did, she learned quite a bit about their environments and language. This process of welcoming others into her environment enhanced her adaptability and reinforced her wisdom pathway. Pretty soon she was asked to be the liaison at outside events. These events were unfamiliar environments to her, attended by very wealthy and important business associates. However, my friend was able to speak their language and engage very comfortably because of the practice she'd had with similar people who came into her office.

In addition, by connecting with these business associates, both in her office environment and at events, she helped her firm maintain a strong network of investors.  This is an example of how small efforts create a ripple effect. It starts with noticing how others adapt when they enter your environment. And then taking the initiative to welcome them.

---

**SMALL TASK:** *notice other people. How do others interact in your environment.? Even if they come there often, notice if they are comfortable. If someone new comes into your environment, how can you make them feel comfortable?*

---

**SECTION 3**

# Learn

"Learning without thought is labor lost; thought without learning is perilous." **- CONFUCIUS**

"Wisdom is not the product of schooling but of the lifelong attempt to acquire it."

**-ALBERT EINSTEIN**

WISDOM IS NOT ABOUT having all the answers or all the knowledge, it's about knowing you don't *and* that not having all the knowledge and all the answers is okay. Not only is it okay, but it's also imperative. When you learn, you exercise your brain. This keeps your brain functioning optimally. When you stop learning your brain atrophies, just like your muscles when they are not being used.

While it is almost impossible to completely stop learning, it is possible to avoid learning. People avoid learning because they notice just how much there is to learn, and that seems overwhelming and feels uncomfortable. However, to avoid learning is to bring on myriad negative consequences on many neural and physiological levels.

Even when you embrace learning, it can still be overwhelming and uncomfortable. Have you ever attempted to complete a Rubik's Cube? Have you felt that surge of excitement when you get one side nearly or fully completed? Then you turn the cube and realize the other five sides are still out of whack or that you undid the other sides in the process of getting all of one side? There you go, overwhelmed and uncomfortable! And that's just a silly game. Have you ever found this happening in your life? Just when you think you have something figured out you turn a corner and realize not only have you missed something completely, but now you must start from square one? Hopefully, I'm not the only one who would say *yes* to all the above.

While it might seem like I want to include you so that I don't feel like the only dummy out there, I am hoping you said *yes* because that means you are attuned to wisdom. The moment when you are humbled by how little you know and/or how much more there is to learn is a moment of pure wisdom.

I am not telling you that you know nothing right now, or that you should be insecure about how little you know right now. I am also not implying that humility is synonymous with wisdom.  What I am doing is applauding your wisdom in believing in the saying, "You don't know what you don't know," and in your willingness to keep learning despite the effort. In this section I want you to notice how these concepts resonate or not with you. Do they bump up against preconceived notions you have about your own knowledge and about wisdom itself? Be thinking about this as you read on.

# MY DAILY HIGH PERFORMANCE LIST

1. WORK TASK

   Why Important

2. WORK TASK

   Why Important

3. WORK TASK

   Why Important

4. PERSONAL TASK

   Why Important

## 11. POWERS OF YOUTH AND AGING

WHEN I ASK MOST PEOPLE, WHAT IMAGE arises when I say the word *wisdom,* or I ask them to picture a wise person, the most frequent characteristic they name is old age. This makes sense because we assume by the end of a lifetime we will have seen and done enough to have wisdom. However, when I ask, "Is every old person also wise?" I get a much different response. Most people agree that not ALL old people are wise. This might be in part because the term "old person" is pretty vague and tends to change depending on the age of the person I am asking. Tell a ninety-year-old that you are seventy, and they'll call you a youngster. It's also because not everyone who has lived into their elderly years has actively sought wisdom. They may have a lot of knowledge and experience, but again, is that the same as wisdom? I say no.

So, is age a necessary precursor of wisdom? Well, this is where it gets interesting. There are certain developmental stages that everyone goes through. Each stage tends to occur during a certain period or age span. The stages of development are predictable, however, the exact age in which they are experienced is not, especially once we move beyond the physical and mental development of youth. The early stages of development in babies, children and teens are more predictable and consistent than those of adulthood. In adulthood, some people may develop and learn much more quickly than others. They move on to the next stage while others linger in a stage and experience it in different ways before they move to the next. Neither way is right or wrong. Speed is not the goal. Everyone can gain wisdom throughout each stage of development by being conscious and deliberate in what and how they learn in any moment.

The goal is to witness and experience each stage fully. This comes back to that Rubik's Cube. Don't assume you know. Instead, be open to what you can learn. By seeking the learning of everything you experience, you absorb knowledge and build a process of being in a place of wisdom at every stage of your life.

Some might find it becomes easier to be in this place of wisdom after they have enough life experience to gain perspective on things. While others may find it more difficult to gain perspective, and therefore wisdom, because their thought patterns have restricted their views. The saying "you can't teach an old dog new tricks" is indicative of the latter. Ultimately, the ability to gain wisdom comes from actively seeking opportunities in small moments in all stages of life, not just waiting it out until you go grey.

One of the best ways to be an active seeker is to think differently as to who you seek wisdom from. It is highly valuable to ask those who are a stage or two beyond you to teach you some of the things they have learned. Seek mentors to help guide your process, someone older (not necessarily "old") who you idolize in some way and learn from them.

However, if much of your time and effort is spent only with those who are older than you, who will still be around to attend your funeral? Meaning, what value do you both gain and offer to those younger than you? Consider mentoring someone who is a stage or two below you as well. Our own learning is solidified when we teach it to others. The teaching process pulls information through the brain in different ways, creating new brain patterns and reinforcing the knowledge.

And I wouldn't stop there. As we agreed, wisdom is not synonymous with old age and old age is not the only time to enter a state of wisdom. If all you ever do is look at those ahead of you for information, all you will get is information about what they have seen and done. These experiences are guided in part by the generation they grew up in and includes the learning necessary to survive and thrive in that particular society. The experiences of each generation vary significantly. Therefore, placing your focus on learning from those older than you is risking the chance that you will create a gap between yourself and those younger than you.

In addition, a past focus places you at risk for missing opportunities to learn about the current society in which you live, and the one that will support you in the future. For example, how many elderly people do you know who don't use computers or cell phones? In the technology age things move and change extremely fast so it is vital to keep up. And who better to teach you than someone who grew up with technology. In addition, young people have an energy and vitality that is contagious. Remember that circle of influence and the significant impact it has on the statistics of your life? If your circle is comprised only of wise old people, it might enhance your wisdom but what does it do for your vitality? Your endurance? Your physique?

When I spend even just a few hours coaching my U-14 soccer team I leave feeling youthful. I feel peppy and sometimes even giddy. The energy and enthusiasm they bring is wonderful, and I absorb it fully so I can keep my own youthfulness alive and inspired. I love learning from them. They have a lot of knowledge and wisdom. I learn new ways to interact, communicate, connect and even new ways to learn.

**SMALL TASK:** *pick your mentors. Seek out two mentors, one younger than you and one older, who actively come from a place of wisdom. Set a date to visit with them. Decide what aspects you specifically want to learn from them. Notice what being around them does for you.*

## 12. EXTRA, EXTRA READ ALL ABOUT IT!

IGNORANCE IS BLISS. It's true, I know. I lived on an isolated island for three years knowing very little about the rest of the world. There was something wonderful about having zero clue as to what was happening; every day I lived in this little postcard bubble caring only about when I should put on more sunscreen.

This chapter is not about reliving my island adventures. That's a different book. It is, however, about the downside of ignorance. In living in my bubble, I missed out on a lot of important information, and some opportunities to be in a state of wisdom. When I came back to the States I had to play catch up, just so I could hold even superficial conversations about current events. I don't enjoy being clueless. It got very old very fast to have someone say, "Did you hear about ____?" and I could only respond, "Uh, no, tell me about it." That response works well maybe once in a conversation, but after two or three times, people start to look at you like you're an idiot. Sadly, I am speaking from experience.

No doubt, there is a lot of bad and negative information out there. I am not advocating that you be glued to the news. However, it is important to have knowledge of both the negative news and the positive news. And there is a lot of good and positive information. There are plenty of stories relating the best of humankind and that demonstrate the expansion of wisdom in our society. And there is innovation occurring all over the world: new ideas, new research, inventions, etc. It's quite staggering.

With all the positive news out there, why not just pay attention to the good and avoid the bad? Because if we all simply ignored the bad news, we may not be motivated to create something new.  Where do you think all the innovation stems from? Typically, it doesn't occur when everything is flowing smoothly, and everyone is having a joyful time. Unfortunately, it tends to stem from when things are not working well, when there is suffering or dysfunction or corruption.

While you personally may not aspire to be an innovator, having awareness about what is going on in the world (the good and the bad) is still vital to your ability to connect with others. It creates opportunities to understand and relate to others. For example, you may have no connection to or interest in politics, however, the person next to you might have a lot of interest in this subject. They might even be allowing this information to consume them, causing them stress, and suffering in their daily interactions. By learning about the world around you, you are better prepared to understand the world of others, and how they are guiding their experiences by what they choose to focus on.

Taking time to learn about the world is a big and global as well as a small and local task. This knowledge both big and small may impact your future in various ways, if none other than to give you more choices. When you have awareness about your surroundings, you can predict and be strategic in your planning rather than reactive.

This information will guide you in making many decisions. This could be anything and everything from long term financial investments, to choosing local farm share options, or even getting involved in your local

HOA making decisions regarding the color of your front door. The point is, learning about both your local world and your global world can build your state of wisdom. And wisdom dictates that you will be an active seeker and an active chooser, as opposed to an ignorant reactor.

---

**SMALL TASK:** *information is your friend. Seek out information about the world today. Learn something news-related AND something innovation related. They do not need to be in the same area or topic. Just learn and notice if this new awareness causes you to think differently about your immediate situation. Does it cause a shift in your physical or mental state? Does it make you want to learn even more?*

## 13. ALL THESE USEFUL GADGETS

IN THE LAST CHAPTER, I talked briefly about youth and innovation. Younger generations don't know life without technology. When my nephew was two years old, I gave him my phone to play with. I was still using a Blackberry. Yes, I was slow to get with the times. He had only seen an iPhone. By two years old he knew how to enter the password to my sister's iPhone, click on pictures and videos and blow up the screen by spreading his fingers. When he took my Blackberry, which had none of those capabilities, he looked at me with a look that said, "Is there a reason you prefer to stay in the stone age?" Then he promptly handed it back to me.

He's now five years old and has a Skylander toy that includes a chip in the bottom that serves as a game. You place the plastic toy on a receiver, and it pulls up a game portal on the TV specific to that character. Each character has its own embedded game with choose-your-own-adventure scenarios. This is a far cry from the Atari pinball and Duck Hunt games I remember. Children's toys are now layered with technology that 20 years ago would have been reserved for those with advanced degrees, special training, and lots of money.

Though I use video games as an example, it is not to initiate the debate about whether they rot your brain. It is simply to highlight kids are growing up in a technology world. Their brains are wired differently from ours. They are not afraid to push the buttons and see what happens. They are primed to poke and prod and to figure out how things work. They are primed to find easier and faster solutions. This is an incredible advantage, and we can learn so much from them. They are teaching us that it's not about having the right answers but about asking the right questions. When we embrace technology, we open a whole new avenue for learning.

You know you are becoming an "old dog" when you balk at learning how to use yet another new technology. This resistance is a natural response to getting off your autopilot pattern and doing something new. Making this switch is more effortful than just doing what you have always done. But the likelihood is that your old way was probably less efficient, hence the new technology. So, catch yourself. When you have an "old dog" thought or resistance, slap the back of your hand and say, "bad dog," then open yourself up to learning.

Technology is everywhere, there is no escaping it, and it is probably making your life better. Let's embrace it! If keeping up with technology is difficult, use it as an opportunity to widen your circle of influence to include a few tech-savvy young people.

---

**SMALL TASK:** *learn something new about the technology around you. Embrace this technology, see if you are maximizing its capabilities and functions. Do you have your Outlook synced fully? Do you have your documents sorted and saved to the cloud? Have you explored Google docs? Notice how innovative and efficient our society has become and how it truly can help you be more efficient and productive!*

## 14. BOOK WORM

IN TAKING MY OWN ADVICE about embracing technology, I bought a Kindle. However, I will always own printed books, even though I get annoyed every time I move, and I must drag the book boxes with me. I do have a caveat about my Kindle: I only use it for leisure reading books. There is a very important reason for this. When I read a book to learn, I prefer a printed copy. With a printed book, I can highlight, write notes in the margins, flip back through it for references, and refresh my knowledge. I don't do this just for fun. Highlighting, writing notes, and revisiting the content are vital tools to retaining and learning information.

Did you know you only retain ten percent of what you read? If you add notetaking to what you have read that percentage goes up to 50 percent. If you read, take notes, and talk to someone else about what you read, your retention goes up to 70 percent. Now apply that information to real life situations (practice using it) and your retention of the original printed information rises to 90 percent.

How's that possible? When you take in information visually, via reading, you are using a specific area of your brain. When you write about that information you shift to a different region of your brain. Then when you speak about that information you shift to yet another region of your brain. All this shifting around is effortful for the brain and creates new neural pathways, which reinforces the retention of information. This is what causes that 10 percent retention to jump to 90 percent.

And the effort your brain must apply to transfer that information to new areas exercises your brain, making it stronger and more resilient.

There is another reason why it is important to pull the information through many different regions of your brain: to move that knowledge to long term memory. The space in your conscious working memory (short term memory) is very limited. Because the space is limited and so much information is constantly coming in, information only lasts there a few seconds. By processing information through different regions of your brain and accessing it often, the information shifts into long-term memory. Now your brain can apply it and advancing that information in novel ways. Congratulations, you have workable knowledge about that subject.

To adapt, connect, learn, and be present in the moment it is necessary to have a very active and resilient brain. Reading is a great start, but adding various sensory components is even better.  You will also gain flexibility and awareness of opportunities to seize.

So, read often, read lots of different authors and genres. Be open to new ideas, new data, new research, and new opinions. Read the memoirs, biographies, and stories of those you look up to. Actively engage with the information. Highlighting meaningful passages, taking notes, and talking about the information suggests that you are curious and are thinking about how you will use the information, and how it might be relevant to others. Sounds like wisdom in action to me

**SMALL TASK:** *create a book list. And not just books. Include at least 10-2 books/writings/articles/studies. Make time today to read. Add reading to your daily routine, even if only for 20 minutes per day. Make a note or two about what you read and share a bit of it with someone else.*

## 15. MIRROR, MIRROR ON THE WALL

HAVE YOU EVER HEARD that history repeats itself? The idea behind this truism comes from philosopher George Santayana who in his 1905 book, *The Life of Reason*, wrote, "Those who do not remember the past are doomed to repeat it." Since then, it's been shown that even those who remember the past are doomed to repeat it.  This is because remembering is not enough. We must remember, learn from it, and choose a different course of action. So, why don't we?

I have mentioned our brain's amazing ability to be energy efficient by creating habits or reinforced pathways that fire automatically in response to specific triggers. Once a pattern or pathway is automated it can be difficult to realize it's being activated because it no longer requires your prefrontal cortex or thinking brain to fire. Instead, the pattern now resides in your mid-brain, which means it can be fired without you consciously triggering it. This is why you can tie your shoes and hold a conversation at the same time. Your shoe tying ability is automated, so it no longer requires your attention.

The dangers of this function are that these automated pathways are not just reserved for mindless tasks and hygiene. They occur in all areas of our lives including patterns in thinking, patterns in communicating, patterns in feeling, patterns in managing stress, etc. Furthermore, these patterns exist in societies and determine how we remember the past and how we choose to act in the present.

Because these patterns are stored in the subconscious brain we don't notice when they are triggered. To do so requires tracking and reflecting. I won't attempt to explain how societies can be wiser by making these conscious efforts. Instead, for now, I'll just focus on individuals.

First, choose an area in your life that is not working for you. To track it, write down why it's not working, and whether what is going on has happened before, and how often. Next (and this is the hard part) reflect on what *your* role is in this situation. In other words, what patterns are you executing and what are the triggers?

Reflecting on our roles is difficult because sometimes we are in situations that we cannot control, or we attribute the cause to something external. Unfortunately, when we place the cause outside ourselves, we become the victim who must simply endure. I had a work situation like this a few years back. My boss was a tyrant who thrived on making everyone feel small and miserable. I convinced myself that the situation was hopeless and that there was nothing I could do about changing him. Every week I would go to the same staff meeting and every week I would walk away pulling my hair out. This went on for months. Clearly something was not working.

Finally, I decided to reflect on *my* role and *my* patterns. This required effort and willingness to look at myself in the mirror. I had to be willing to take ownership of my own reactions and my own patterns. As I tracked my reactions, I began to connect my thought patterns to my feelings. I knew I had to change my thoughts so that I would feel differently.

I realized while I cannot change him, nor would I want to expend that much energy on someone so terrible, I could control my reactions. I could change my emotional pattern of frustration that was triggered every time he walked in the room. I did this by adding a new thought to trigger a new emotion and reaction. I created a new pattern that allowed me to stay calm and balanced in his presence.

Once I opened that door of self-reflection, I also noticed the positive patterns I was executing. For example, I recognized how this "bad boss" situation triggered me to connect more with my team. I was extra considerate and active in making sure the team morale stayed high and everyone felt supported. My efforts instigated everyone on the team to respond to each other more kindly and effectively. With new awareness, I deliberately reinforced a new pattern by making even more effort to boost morale and team unity.

Reflecting is a powerful tool. It should be done regularly. Whether you want to change something or not, you can only know what processes, patterns and strategies are working if you take time to reflect on them. This doesn't just pertain to reflecting on your thoughts and noticing how they drive your emotions and reactions.  You can practice reflection in other ways. For example, check your time management weekly or monthly to see if you are budgeting your time effectively. Check your bank account every few days to see if you are budgeting your money effectively. Check your goals for the year to see if you are achieving what you set out to do. Reflect and learn what patterns you want to repeat and which ones you want to change.

**SMALL TASK:** *time management. Reflect on your time management so far this week. Are you getting everything done and giving yourself time to rejuvenate? Are you procrastinating and putting off the things you enjoy? Notice your patterns. Which ones have come up before? What are you willing to take control of and change for the better?*

# Balance

"Your hand opens and closes, opens and closes. If it were always a fist or always stretched open, you would be paralyzed. Your deepest presence is in every small contracting and expanding, the two as beautifully balanced and coordinated as birds' wings."

**– JALALUDDIN RUMI**

THIS QUOTE REFERS TO the importance of balance and highlights that balance does not mean lack of movement. It also highlights that balance is not present at all times in all ways, because this simply is not possible. The quote refers to the process of moving in and out of balance, recognizing when you are not in balance and understanding how and when to come back into balance.

In the practice of Hatha yoga, there are many balance poses. Most yoga teachers know that these poses are not about staying perfectly still. Instead, balance poses teach you how to embrace and activate the subtle movements in your body and environment that bring you into balance, or as they might say, harmony. This process of coming into a state of balance is just as vital to learn as being in balance. As a matter of fact, it is doubtful you will find balance and sustain it if you don't understand the process.

Surprisingly, the first step in the process entails recognizing when you are off balance. You must be mindful of when you move away from balance, and of how far you stray before you can ignite efforts (movements) that will bring you back into balance. If you stray too far, those efforts may move from subtle and easy to harsh and time consuming. For example, overindulging in work and restricting sleep for too long may result in full-blown flu as opposed to a mild cold. Or worse, what happens to those who spend years overindulging in crappy food, jamming too many to-dos into every day, avoiding exercise, rest and laughter? They wind up with major physical and mental health problems, plus brain fog, loss of friends, weight gain, premature aging, etc. There are so many repercussions of living in imbalance.

Balance is critical to longevity and wellness. And like wisdom, it is not something you achieve and then you are done. There are many components to a balanced life, and they are often personal and individualized. However, in general, there are some strategies that we all can benefit from including morning routines, daily organization, mid-day recovery and lots and lots of laughter.

By implementing the strategies in this section, you will be better able to maximize the staples of good health: time, nutrition, movement and sleep. These staples are weaved into each chapter with regards to how and when the strategies can be applied.

## 16. FIRST OFF THE BLOCK

IN THE SPORT OF TRACK & FIELD the athlete who is first off the block has the advantage. This can be applied to all our lives; how you start your day matters. Ask anyone who has their life on track, is very accomplished, is highly productive, and has a high level of life balance and they will likely say they have an effective routine for how they start their day.

We've all had days that started off chaotically and had us chasing our tails the rest of the day. Some of us leave this to chance while others choose to prevent these occasions by using deliberate routines. Starting your day effectively doesn't guarantee a perfect day, just like being first off the block doesn't guarantee a win. However, a routine does set you up to have success more often than not and gives you an advantage.

One of the best things you can do to maximize effort and energy is to create effective routines. Routines cause our brains to develop highly grooved pathways that become automated. When this happens, the tasks involved in the routine take much less effort to perform, which saves us energy. For example, some people lay their gym clothes out before bed, and in the morning, they put them on and immediately go to the gym. They don't lie in bed in the morning and question whether they will go to the gym. They just get up, thoughtlessly put their gym clothes on, and go. Their routine has just about guaranteed that they will stick with their goal of being more fit.

Routines also activate desired states of mind. Let's say when you are executing your routine you notice a feeling: content, happy, energized, etc. By engaging in that routine, the same way every day (which is the definition of a routine), you reinforce the feeling state associated with it. Elite athletes know this process well. For example, when a baseball player has a routine of taking three practice swings before stepping into the batter's box, he initiates a state of "confidence." Doing this routine the same way every time the athlete triggers that "confidence" state every time. This "confidence" state allows the athlete's mind and body to be focused and agile, which makes him more likely to hit the 90 miles per hour fastball coming at him.

Routines are really powerful, so be careful. When we don't create deliberate routines, we may fall into ineffective habits. For example, if you hit the snooze button 18 times every morning then jump out of bed in a cranky hurry, guess what state you activate by continuing to engage in that same process? By allowing the routine to continue it further reinforces the state associated with it and increases the likelihood you will keep doing that same ineffective process.

The good news is, if you've already created an adverse routine, it can be changed. It takes effort and consistency to automate a new process and drive a new state activation. However, soon enough the routine will be your new habit.

Routines are not just ideal for morning time. We are engaging in routines throughout our entire day. Some are deliberate and effective, while others aren't really serving us well at all. Consider what routines you follow throughout your day. Are they effective? Do they trigger a positive state? Could you benefit from a few more deliberate routines?

**SMALL TASK:** *effective routines. Enhance your morning with a routine. What steps will you follow from the moment you open your eyes? How do you like to feel when you start your optimal day? How can you trigger that state first thing in the morning? Make this your routine and notice how you feel moving forward.*

## 17. PUT IT ON A POST-IT

HAVE YOU HEARD THE SAYING that a cluttered room makes for a cluttered mind? To this I would say yes and no. It really depends on your definition of clutter. In my office, for example, I have what is called an organized mess. To some, including my office mate (who is a neat freak by the way), my desk seems messy, but to me it's organized in a way that works well for me. I know exactly where everything is and why one item is placed in one pile while another item is in a different pile. And I use the word pile loosely because a pile implies that they are neatly stacked, and mine are not. But I have a reason why the pile is askew. For me, if it's out of sight it's out of mind, so my piles are set in such a way that I can see some part of everything in the pile. And I like driving my office mate crazy.

However, even I have my limits. And you should too because there is a limit to how much chaos or clutter a brain can handle. The average conscious working memory can only process seven "things" at a time (plus or minus two). This means at the high end of the range you can hold nine "things" in your awareness at any one time, and on the low end of the range you can hold five "things" in your awareness at any one time.

Think of your working memory as a standard post-it note. That's about the capacity of your conscious awareness in any given moment. In order for your brain to keep up, it simply slides one "thing" off the list to add the newest priority "thing." Ever go to the grocery store and come home without the milk? You walked out the door repeating the list in your head, "Milk, cheese, butter, eggs, bread, ...milk, cheese, butter, eggs, bread ...milk, cheese, butter, eggs, bread..." But then your spouse called and asked for wine. Now your list sounds more like, "Wine.... bread... eggs... bread... cheese wine..." The milk promptly slid off the list and the wine became the newest priority. Not a big problem when it's just milk. But what about when you are missing important deadlines, forgetting to pay a bill, or showing up late to your child's recital? These things happen when your day, your calendar and your desk are overloaded with chaos and clutter.

The brain is a highly organized structure. To make sense of the world and operate efficiently, the brain sorts all incoming information into organized categories. You can make this work easy for your brain, or you can make it hard depending on how organized you are. I'm not saying that your world must be neat and tidy at all times; life is messy. But the more you can organize your mess, the better for your brain. And you will likely feel the difference as well.

For example, I need an organizational system that doesn't include being neat and tidy because neat and tidy to me equals things out of mind. If you saw my office, you would see a very busy place with tons of post-it notes taped to all the walls in specific sectioned areas. If you didn't understand my system, it would probably take you an hour to make sense of it all. But it does make sense. Priority items are out and highly visible. I rearrange and weed out my space often. I cycle through each item to be sure I haven't missed anything. This process often reignites old ideas, makes room for new ones, and clears off items that I've already addressed or completed. And I feel calmer and more energized every time I complete this process.

Organization goes beyond the office space. It's beneficial in all areas of life, because when you are organized you create space for new and better "things" to enter.  If you are a natural organizer, you might be thinking, "Duh." But if you are like me, it's daunting. I had to figure out an organizational process that could work for me in all areas of my life. To succeed, I adapted the organization routine I use in my office space for use in my closet and kitchen spaces. I also use it to organize my work and exercise schedules.

You can start getting organized by first examining your organization processes. Recognize if you are taking on too many "things." Assess your priorities, not just your to-dos. Which 7 +/-2 things are taking up your day? What if you prioritized them by importance and did the most valuable first? Now think about how you can create or enhance routines to better organize your life. Maybe you incorporate a priority list as a part of your daily routine. Perhaps you could work out in the morning rather than the evening. Perhaps you would spend a few more quality moments really engaging with your family at breakfast. Maybe you only spend 20 minutes on emails in the morning rather than an hour.

If you can't seem to get organized by yourself, ask a friend (or your business partner) for help. It might even be worth it to hire an organization expert. The key is to start small. If that overwhelms you go even smaller. Pick one thing, one area, to start with and when you've mastered that, add another strategy. Watch your new organization habits snowball, and the benefits ripple through your life.

Here's the bottom line. When you introduce effective organization habits you are more likely to remain present and balanced. As a result, your ability to optimally think and function in any given moment increases. This includes your ability to notice and seize opportunities to achieve wisdom in those moments.

**SMALL TASK:** *prioritize. Start your workday by creating a priority list; include time to organize your desk. Notice how it feels to be organized. Notice this increases your productivity, focus and creativity. Create a routine you can tick to that will help you maintain this organization pathway.*

## 18. GIMME A BREAK

OH, THE POWER OF A LUNCH BREAK! A lunch break is a very powerful part of your day, if you use it wisely. This doesn't mean increasing your work output by eating while you catch up on emails. Rather, your lunch break is a golden opportunity to recharge and recover. Our brains are hard at work processing, thinking, reacting, producing, creating, etc. all day long. Imagine if you worked your biceps like you do your brain. Thinking would be synonymous to a bicep curl. How tired might that poor bicep be by lunchtime let alone the end of the day? If you answered, "Pretty dang tired," I would agree. While your brain can handle and endure much more activity than your bicep, it still needs rest.

Lunch is when you refuel with food, and this requires effort from the non-thinking part of your brain. If at the same time you're requiring effort from the thinking part of your brain on some unrelated tasks, you can overload your system. And neither part may work as well as they could. Believe it or not we cannot multi-task with 100% efficiency. When we attempt to put our attention on two different tasks simultaneously our performance drops to 70% *at best* on each individual task.

You may be thinking, "My digestion does not require my attention." This is true. Digestion occurs without you thinking about it. However, digestion is enhanced when you do focus on it, and your brain is less activated when you give it this singular focus. This focus blocks other distracting thoughts from wasting your energy. In turn, this allows you to nourish your body more fully, which refuels your energy, and gives your brain a chance to rest.

Consider this: how thoroughly are you tasting and chewing your food when you engage in a working lunch? Did you know chewing activates saliva, which is your body's first phase of digestion? If you don't take the time to chew, you cause your body to work harder during the subsequent phases of digestion. Could this be a cause of your indigestion and discomfort after you scarf down lunch in a hurry? Could it also be the cause of that afternoon energy slump?

Conversely, consider the other task you are attempting to do while eating. Your ability to hold your attention on this task is compromised. Like I said, when we attempt to multi-task our performance drops to, at best, 70 percent.  If this were a school grade you would be looking at a C. This drops even lower when you attempt to do more than two tasks at a time.

Let's take a closer look at how this plays out. Imagine being in a routine of living one chaotic day after the next. You're constantly chasing the eight-ball and are doing everything you can just to get by. Or at least you think you are. But in fact, by trying to multitask you aren't doing anything really well. You cram every ounce of your day with to-dos, and end up giving a half-assed effort because, quite frankly, you are too darn tired to care anymore. You just want to get home so you can rest. When you get home, you feel like you are living a mediocre life and have no control to change it.

What if, instead, you took one hour in the middle of your day for a time out, to pause, to stop. You refuel your energy by enjoying good food. You sit quietly or maybe go for a walk. This one hour refuels your energy, refocuses your mind and allows you to feel like you are in control again. When you return from lunch, you focus on one task that you give your full attention and effort to. You complete it to the best of your ability, and you feel a small boost of pride because you did good work. Now when you get home at the end of the day you have some energy to be present, to enjoy your dinner and your family or friends. You feel relaxed knowing you are living a great life and can easily maintain it.

I vote for the latter scenario. Furthermore, I vote for your taking your lunch break away from the office. How often have you attempted to sit peacefully in your office, at your desk, in the break room, etc. to eat and were sucked back into working before you could even take your first bite? Yep, I have been there too. Getting away from the office can solve that problem. In addition, leaving the office activates body movement, gets fresh air into your lungs, and changes the scenery, all of which enhance brain function and increase creativity.

When you take the time during lunch to recover, and literally think of your lunch break as a recovery break, your body will refuel more effectively, your brain will get a much-needed break, and your energy will be restored. Now you are ready to hit the afternoon agenda running, ready to think, create, and engage.

**SMALL TASK:** *take a real break. Take a lunch break today away from the office. Go get some fresh air, walk for a few minutes enroute to dining. Really enjoy eating your lunch. Activate your taste buds. Sit back, let your mind relax. Notice how you feel afterwards. Do you feel relaxed? Recharged? Do you have more clarity? Endurance? Patience? My guess is, yes, on all accounts.*

## 19. RED LIGHT, GREEN LIGHT

HAVE YOU EVER AWAKENED the day after Thanksgiving saying, "I'm going to stop overeating!" only to gorge on leftovers hours later? Or woken up after a few too many beers or glasses of wine thinking, "Never again!" knowing full well you will be at next week's happy hour? You are not alone. When you attempt to stop a behavior, especially one that you do often, your effort often fails. There are many reasons why your good intention fell to the wayside, and one of the most influential reasons has to do with the way your brain processes information.

Your brain is very efficient, and it responds very quickly to triggers in your environment. The more you are exposed to that trigger the more highly grooved that pathway becomes. Food is a huge trigger.  For example, you feel hungry, so you head to the break room having the intention to eat a healthy snack. But the break room has daily donuts right out on the counter. It's the first thing you see, so you eat donuts instead of something healthy. This behavior is not serving you, but you keep on doing it anyway, because the donuts are always there, and you now associate hunger satisfaction with donuts.

Once a pathway reaches the point of automation, it is now a habit. Most people think that to stop this habit you need willpower. Just stop eating the donuts! However, stop behaviors don't work because your brain doesn't actually stop firing neural pathways. It simply fires alternate ones. If you aren't deliberate in directing these alternate pathways you will go right back to the donuts, or something similar. The best way to stop this habit is to add a start behavior (deliberate direction of an alternate pathway), that in time will replace the old habit with a new habit.

So, back to the donut example. Don't fret about eating the donut. Eat an apple first. In doing this you disrupt the physiological link between hunger satiation and donuts with a new neural pathway. This works even if you want to make huge shifts in your eating habits. For example, if you want to eat better in general, it won't work to tell yourself to, "Stop eating all junk food." Instead, add more healthy foods, and eat the healthy foods *before* the foods you normally eat. Start with a salad and a glass of water before you dive into the chili cheese fries. This will begin to disrupt the habit of eating unhealthy foods. Eventually, you will eat less of the unhealthy stuff and more of the good foods your body really needs. The key is to be deliberate and plan what you will add and when.

Adding start behaviors that benefit you is a great way to shift your habits in a sustainable way. Start behaviors initiate alternate pathways, give you a sense of control, and prevent the negative self-talk or guilt thoughts associated with failed stop behaviors. You are less likely to beat yourself up for eating the chili cheese fries if you eat a salad first. And you are less likely to eat as many fries if you already put something healthy in your stomach.

This start behavior process doesn't just apply to your eating habits. Any habit you notice that does not serve you can be shifted. However, nutrition is a great place to practice initiating start behaviors simply because we can always eat better or add more healthy foods. When you practice adding a start behavior process it will become easier and more automatic to do this consciously in all other areas of your life.

---

**SMALL TASK:** *start behaviors. Add a start behavior to your nutrition. Start each meal with a glass of water or add a side salad or side of fruit to lunch or dinner. Notice how easy this is and how it enhances positive self-talk and optimism. Practice this consistently and notice how the unwanted habits shift.*

---

## 20. A CASE OF THE GIGGLES

LAUGHTER IS POWERFUL. It is also highly underrated. In fact, it's even looked down upon in some cases. If you laugh too much or dare to have fun at work, what would people think? It is simply not professional, right? Wrong. Laughter needs to be taken more seriously. Laughter is the key to youth, creativity, good health, and of course, balance.

Laughter is contagious. Have you ever watched a laughter reel and not laughed? I love the ones with babies laughing, it gets me every time! Next time you are in a bad mood, YouTube a laughter reel and see what happens to your mood.

There is a body of research on the effects of laughter on your health and well-being. In a previous chapter, I talked about the un-doing effect of gratitude on stress responses. Laughing also has an un-doing effect. Laughter has been shown to reduce blood pressure, reduce depression, increase blood circulation, and boost your immune system, just to name a few. And the more you laugh, the more you groove those pathways; you laugh more readily and enhance the un-doing effects even more. And because laughter is contagious, when you laugh others laugh with you, triggering their own un-doing effect.

What's more, it doesn't have to be genuine laughter. Just faking laughter can ignite this ripple effect. When you fake laugh, you activate the same muscles in your face and throat as real laughter, which causes the same physiological response. Also, fake laughter leads to real laughter. There is a specific type of yoga predicated on this process. It is aptly called laughter yoga. In this practice, you initiate laughter through a series of fake or modeled laughter type breaths. The modeled laughter breath triggers real laughter. This shift is felt on a physiological level. The research on laughter yoga shows an immediate improvement in mental, emotional, and physical states after just one session.

You do not need to enroll in a laughter yoga class to experience these benefits. Actively seeking moments of laughter in your day is just as valuable. However, I suggest being deliberate, especially if laughter is infrequent in your day. Remember, laughing initiates the un-doing effect of stress responses, allows you to move back to center, back into balance, and may prevent you from straying past the point of no return.

Those who recognize the importance of laughter in their lives and make a conscious effort to laugh daily, are truly wise.

---

**SMALL TASK:** *schedule time to laugh today. Plan three times today to trigger laughter, even for a few moments. Watch a funny video, picture a funny memory, tell a funny story. Notice how you feel after laughing. Practice this consistently and notice if you can maintain amusement throughout your day. Notice even more opportunities to laugh every day.*

# Purpose

"I don't want to be the one who says life is beautiful, I want to be the one who feels it."

**– MARTY RUBIN**

THIS QUOTE REMINDS ME of purpose because it's about accessing a state of being, not about something outside of myself. When you connect to your purpose, it resonates internally and emanates into your external world.  Sounds magical, doesn't it?  But connecting to this state is not as hard as it sounds. And, once you experience this powerful state, it changes your perspective. Connecting with your purpose creates a focus to everything you do. It is your reason for doing what you do. With your purpose in mind, what was once hard is now easy, and what is truly important to you is clearly seen. Knowing your purpose also gives you permission to remove senseless stuff, habits, and even people from your life.

I don't want to give the impression that you only have one purpose. Because again, connecting with your purpose is about accessing a state of being. You may have multiple purposes at one time, or different purposes at different times of your life. Connecting with your purpose can entail simple or complex tasks and have short- or long-term goals.

Purpose is not synonymous with goal achievement, although they are closely linked. Being overly focused on the outcome of the goal, however, can draw you away from your purpose, and ultimately, from wisdom. However, if you seek the process of pursuing a goal *as* the outcome, then you will stay connected to your purpose, and to your wisdom. The more often you practice this process the more likely you are to achieve many wonderful, even limitless goals.

There are many ways of connecting to your purpose and leveraging your purpose to initiate actions. In these next chapters, I'll focus on five specific strategies: imagery, challenging your challenges, maintaining motivation, reframing, and celebration.

## 21. LOOK FOR THE LIGHTHOUSE

A LIGHTHOUSE IS A BEACON, a light in the distance that helps guide a ship towards the shore. The beacon is out in the distance. It is something to tune into that lets you know that you are on target to reach a goal, in this case the shore. Let's refer to your purpose as your lighthouse with a beacon that guides you to reach your goals. Your goal may be to clean out the garage or run a marathon; the goal itself doesn't matter to the lighthouse. The lighthouse (your purpose) represents a state of being, and a focus to all that you do.

People who know their purpose typically feel a sense of thriving in everything that they do. When I operate from a state of purpose, I feel limitless and energized. I am in tune with my body. I know exactly how to shift into balance and stay present. I am active and fit. I feel strong, limber, and ageless. This state is not a result of achieving my goals of cleaning the garage or running a marathon. It's rather what guides me to achieve those goals; I may choose to run marathons because of being in this state and living from this state. Do you see the difference?

When you identify your state, describe it in a detailed way (as I did above). When you live from a state of thriving, for example, how will you feel? How will you think? What words or phrases will you speak often? Who and what is there with you? What is the environment? What can you see, feel, hear, taste, and smell when you are living in this way? Practice vividly imagining this state, incorporating the details of each sense into that imagery. By doing so, you create the neural pathways that can ignite the state at any time, just by imagining it.

Elite athletes use this imagery strategy all the time, and its effectiveness has been well documented. When those imagery pathways fire, they activate a chain of physiological responses through your body, even activating your muscles. This means if you are a runner and vividly imagine a trail you often run on, then you will ignite the same state and the same muscles that you feel and use when you are actually running that trail. Your brain cannot tell the difference between imagined and real. And while an imagined experience is not a replacement for the actual physical execution, it's still a highly valuable tool.

Here's how. When you use imagery, you are actually training your brain to start from the end state to reach any goal you set. Starting from your end state gives you the best vantage point to know exactly what steps you need to take, and what steps are not necessary to reach your goal. You have a well-lit, guided path. Knowing this upfront helps you maximize your energy and effort because the actions you choose will only be those that fall in line with your end state.

And it gets better. The lighthouse image acts as a shortcut to this process. The lighthouse image triggers your brain to ignite your end state without having to go through a ten-minute imagery session of your end state. Once you trigger this state with your lighthouse image, you shift into the feeling place of achievement. Continued use of the image reinforces the brain pathways of your desired end state.

I access my lighthouse as a beacon for achieving every goal. For example, it I decide to run a marathon, even though I never have, just imagining my lighthouse takes me to a state of success. I feel myself there, I can vividly see the people, hear them cheering, I feel my lungs and muscles working hard, I see myself crossing the finish line. In this state, my brain cannot tell the difference between this imagery and reality. All the same pathways, even muscles will fire. Crazy huh? Every time I activate my lighthouse to guide me in reaching my goal, I reinforce the brain pathways that will help me achieve it.

Your lighthouse is your beacon that you can connect to and check in with anytime. Use it as an opportunity to realign and attain your goals. Remember, the lighthouse is not the goal, it is the guide to attaining your goals, with purpose.

---

**SMALL TASK:** *picture your lighthouse. Close your eyes and take three deep breaths. Jump ahead about five years. Congratulations, you are thriving! Imagine how you feel, what you see, what you hear. Who is there with you? What is there around you? What are you doing for a living? How does your body feel? Imagine all the details as if you are really there. Open your eyes and notice how you feel. Connect to this lighthouse three times each day.*

## 22. FROM PEBBLES TO MILESTONES

STEP ONE: SET GOALS. Everyone tells us to set goals, keep our eye on the prize, and keep moving towards the lighthouse. However, we often forget it's also vital to put your head down, look at your feet, and notice where you are

. To attain goals, you must know where you are headed *and* know where you are right now.

Interestingly, to know where you are right now you must know where you've been. When my clients tell me about their goals, however big or small, I ask them, "Why haven't you already achieved it?" I tell them to take a minute and look back. "Where have you been?"

In a past chapter, I talked about building a consistent reflection process into your routine. This is a great way to practice that routine. Reflecting back grounds, you in a very real way to where you are right now *and* highlights the challenges you will likely face again.

When you reflect you will point out many valid reasons why "life" has gotten in the way of you achieving your goals. I say valid because these reasons are not excuses, they are your truths. And because you likely have invested a lot of time and energy into reinforcing the validity of these reasons, it would be fruitless for anyone to pick these reasons apart or challenge them. So, I acknowledge your reasons as real and valid. And I will remind you that history tends to repeat itself. Therefore, you will likely see these "reasons" again as you embark on attaining your next goals. So, let's plan for that.

This entails a small shift in how you approach your goals, and it's immensely effective. For example, instead of waking up on January 1st feeling fresh and thinking, "This year will be different!" (as in, all challenges will fall away or simply not phase me), you will shift to the thought, "This year will be the same, and I will be different." This means that you will plan for those same challenges that have come up time and time again in the past, rather than assume they no longer exist, or will no longer disrupt you.

With your new mindset in place, use the skill of mental contrasting to support it, and to meet challenges to goal achievement head on. Mental contrasting is a brain-based technique proven to

enhance optimism while eliciting potential blocks or challenges.

The contrast is between the benefits of attaining the goal and the obstacles to attaining the goal. Start with writing down a benefit, then write down an obstacle, not to the benefit, but to attaining the goal. For example, a benefit of writing a book will be the feeling of pride I will feel by this achievement. The obstacle to writing the book is that I don't believe I have enough time to write. Now I go back to writing a benefit. Another benefit will be the credibility a book will lend to my reputation and business. And now another obstacle. An obstacle I see is that I don't know how much to charge for a book. These benefits and obstacles are not directly related other than both are being about the goal.

The reason it is important to contrast back and forth between benefits and obstacles is that the process ignites optimism while addressing reality. If you just list the benefits, you are at risk of creating an unrealistic plan. However, if you just list the obstacles, you may talk yourself out of even trying to attain the goal. By jumping back and forth from one to the other you can connect to the end state, maintain optimism, and plan for known obstacles.

Once I have my list, I can set aside the benefits and focus on the obstacles. I use a when/then strategy to address the obstacles with solutions. For example, I had a goal to be a morning exerciser. Each week I would set my intention, and with conviction decide, this is the week! Then the next morning in my half-awake state of impulse I would hit the snooze button. Why? When I reflected on my past attempts to be a morning exerciser, I realized I had convinced myself that I was too tired in the mornings to get up and do it, hence I hit the snooze button.

I couldn't stop hitting the snooze button, day after day after day, month after month. After further analysis, I knew what was preventing me from getting up. I was hitting the snooze button before I could feel alert enough to think about my goals. The reason wasn't that I was too tired (I was getting plenty of good sleep), it was that I was on autopilot. I needed to disrupt this process and to embed a new brain pathway.

So, I created a when/then strategy. I was careful to create a plan with start behaviors, rather than stop behaviors (e.g., stop hitting the snooze button). I set the intention that when the alarm goes off, then I will get up and get dressed. I also interrupted the impulse to hit the snooze button by placing my alarm across the room on my desk, rather than on my bed stand. No analysis or negotiations, just action. By having to get up out of bed to turn off the alarm my old autopilot habit of hitting the alarm was extinguished, as was the thought associated with it: that I was too tired to get up. This plan was very successful, and I am happy to report that I am now a morning exerciser.

The when/then strategy rewires your brain by re-routing the trigger to the existing highly grooved pathway (autopilot). For me, the trigger is the alarm going off. Previously, the trigger would ignite the thought, "I'm tired," which triggered the feeling of being tired, and the impulse to reach over and hit the snooze button. Now that same trigger ignites the impulse to jump up and turn off that noise across the room. This is just enough of a shift to activate the thought, "I am a morning exerciser" (my goal), which ignites a feeling of excitement, and the action to get dressed and go to the gym.

Notice how little effort this shift required. I chose an obstacle that prevented me from achieving my goal in the past and created a very small and easy solution. I did not try to WILL my way through it, which upon failure might cause me to question my identity and self-worth.

In summary, reflect on past patterns to understand where you are now. Contrast benefits and obstacles to your goal. And create a when/then strategy. Seek a shift in thought and behavior that requires the least amount of effort, but that will bring you the biggest return.

---

**SMALL TASK:** *practice mental contrasting. Alternate between a benefit of achieving your goal and a challenge that has or will get in your*

*Create one when/then action plan to re-route you into the action you seek.*

---

## 23. NOW YOU SEE IT...NOW YOU DON'T

EVENTUALLY, THE GARBAGE MAN no longer smells garbage, the packrat no longer sees a mess, and the musician no longer hears the audience talking while she's on stage playing. It's not that their noses and eyes and ears aren't working. Rather their brains have adapted to these sensory inputs so that they are no longer nuisances distracting them from their tasks.

Our brains are great at adapting to the challenges we face regularly, so that we can operate more efficiently. It adapts by putting into autopilot parts of our tasks that don't require attention or thought. Consider the act of brushing your teeth. How much attention or thought do you put into it? How about riding a bicycle? You never forget how, right? But what if you had to teach a child how to ride a bicycle?  You know generalities about the process, but can you explain it step by step? Can you explain how to transfer and balance body weight while building enough momentum to keep moving forward?

The fact is, once a task becomes automated it can be difficult to remember HOW you do it. What does this have to do with motivation? Well, there is a downside to automation. While it may be highly energy efficient it can prevent us from creating new and valuable pathways. We become creatures of habit, doing what we always do rather than doing something different simply because it's easier. It takes less effort mentally and physically. Newton has a well-known law about this.

However, this can be the death of motivation, which can prevent you from achieving or maintaining your goals. Let's say you hang a new picture of your family in your office. This picture is meant to motivate you to stay on task at work so that you don't have to bring work home, which would interfere with your family time. At first, the picture works well. Every time you step into your office it catches your eye because it's a new object that holds special meaning. You see this picture, and it activates a loving feeling. This translates into motivation for you. As a result, you stay on task, get your work done at the office, and enjoy your family time.

However, over time you may find the picture no longer catches your eye. Not because you don't feel motivated by your family, but because your brain has adapted to the sight of the picture and placed it out of conscious awareness. Your brain shifted the décor and layout of your office into your autopilot brain, so you no longer must consider your surroundings. Your brain thinks this is very clever, because now your surroundings won't be a "nuisance" to you and interfere with your accomplishing your tasks. But now your motivation has become automated!

So, here's the conundrum. If we seek to be working, building, and shifting towards wisdom, but our brains like to put us on autopilot, how do we balance the two? Keep your motivation moving. Motivation isn't a one and done, it is ongoing and must be fluid. You must be on your toes. It is important to stay fresh, to stay energized, and actively engaged with the process. Try adding layers of motivators. Add people, places and things that motivate you. Put together a personal cheer squad that can keep you excited and pepped up. Ask some of your skeptic friends or co-workers to keep you in line by calling you out and challenging you to push a little harder.

Use a physical image or symbol of your lighthouse goal or end state. Place it somewhere that you will trip over it often (notice it). Then occasionally move it to another spot, preferably before your brain learns to ignore it. Perhaps make it a game with one of your support people. Let them move it on you periodically. Then when you discover it, you will receive a whole new charge and be reignited. The idea is to move it often so that it continues to be energizing. This symbol should never collect dust. If you do this, you will maintain motivation, build the brain pathways that move you toward your goals, and continue toward wisdom.

---

**SMALL TASK:** *Move your motivation triggers. Rearrange the pictures and symbols in your office. Reignite your motivation. Notice how you feel. Make this shifting of motivation a routine.*

*Rearrange often.*

---

## 24. "IT'S NOT THAT BAD"

WHY DO WE PREFER the short-term, quick fix rather than the long-term satisfaction or gain? Is it because we are all immature or uneducated? Nope. While that may be the case for some, I am guessing if you have picked up this book you are both mature and intelligent. And yet, you may still find yourself sacrificing long term gains for short-term satisfaction. Why? You may have guessed it, that good ol' brain programming.

Energy and effort are mobilized by fear and pleasure. In any given moment, we move toward something that gives us pleasure, or move away from something that causes pain or discomfort (fear). Together with the brain's ability to adapt and desire to maintain balance, a threshold of functioning is created; a top and bottom, so to speak, of where you operate comfortably. Many refer to this as a "comfort zone." I prefer the term "familiar zone" simply because that zone may not be particularly comfortable, yet we continue to stay there because it's familiar, and thus energy efficient to stay there.

Our thoughts are what drive these thresholds. Our thoughts set and maintain our own boundaries for what is possible. We often do this without even realizing it because our thoughts can become patterns, and they are ultimately what trigger our actions. When we come close to the edges of our threshold, we have fear thoughts, which trigger quick fix actions to get us back into a familiar zone, ASAP. This can be a problem when that quick fix action is counter to our long-term goals.

However, there is good news. We can change our thoughts and our thresholds. This change doesn't require hours upon hours of running through the ticker tape of the millions of thoughts we have had over the course of our lives. We can focus on one very specific and powerful statement that provides a direct cue as to why you are struggling to shift, why you are unable to take a new path, why you feel perpetually mediocre, why you are not achieving your goals.

The statement is, "It's not that bad."

When you think or utter the statement, "It's not that bad" you send a signal to your brain that you are okay in your current zone, that you have not bottomed out just yet, and you can stay at this level. Now consider for a minute what would cause you to say (think) such a thing? Is it when you are experiencing something wonderful that is elevating your state of being? Not likely. This statement is reserved for those times you are not "comfortable," but you are trying to convince yourself you can tolerate the discomfort.

The first thing to realize is that, in most cases, we don't make changes when we are comfortable. We make changes when we drop below our comfort threshold. This drop doesn't necessarily mean you've hit rock bottom and are now homeless, drug addicted, hospitalized, or whatever made-for-tv-movie depiction you have of rock bottom. It means you've reached a level of discomfort that you deem unacceptable and unbearable, and you refuse to go any lower.

This is the point when you say, "Oh hell no, I am not buying a size 16," or "Oh hell no, I will NOT stay in this job for the rest of my career." I want you to think about this for a minute and consider your thresholds. Where are you now in relation to what you desire? How much further do you have to go before you drop out of your "familiar zone?" When are you saying to yourself, "It's not that bad?" Now that you have some awareness where you currently stand, let's learn how to leverage the pain/pleasure process to activate movement toward your goals.

You've told yourself, "It's not that bad." This statement causes you to look down. Instead of focusing *up* on the place you would rather be, your attention is *down* while you justify how you aren't quite to the bottom. You are okay and can tolerate staying right where you are. So, your first step is to stop looking down, and start looking up. I'm not talking about thinking happy thoughts. I am talking about reframing what (pain) you are willing to tolerate.

Here are two different ways you can go about reframing. One way is to launch yourself into that black hole of pain so you can finally get motivated to crawl out. For example, some people do this on Thanksgiving. They go all in, gorging themselves, knowing how horrible they will feel. This horrible feeling jars them into a workout streak. While this can be effective, it's very effortful, and entails quite a bit of struggle. And it typically is not a sustainable approach.

The second way to reframe is to go in the opposite direction. Rather than thinking about bringing yourself down to the floor (into the black hole of pain), consider bringing that floor up to you. In essence, reframe your idea of what the bottom is. Rather than convincing yourself that, "It's not that bad," convince yourself why where you are right now *is* that bad. How do you do that? Drama.

Do you watch reality TV of any kind (and want to admit it)? Do you watch movies? We seem to be obsessed with drama. We thrive on drama…other people's drama, that is. We minimize our own drama and tell ourselves, "It's not that bad." We justify our own unwanted situations and talk ourselves into settling and tolerating them. If we do it well enough, we can put off fixing these situations indefinitely, and as a result put off feeling pain over them now.

Right now, you are using drama to negotiate for the enemy (tolerating pain and discomfort). But what if you could use it to negotiate for your best interests (pleasure)? What if you could thrive on your own drama by using it to reframe your "familiar zone?" Here's where you get to dwell in your drama. Make a case for why where you are right now *is* that bad and bring on the drama! Really pull out all the stops, search for all the reasons, all the issues, all the horrible ripples that will occur by NOT acting now.

For example, you head to the break room and notice a box of cupcakes. In your current rationale, whether you realize it or not, the taste or pleasure of a cupcake or cookie is more powerful than the fear of being fat or unhealthy. So, you eat the cupcake (or two). To avoid feeling bad about this, you look down. You convince yourself that being fat and/or unhealthy is not that bad, or that you are not that fat or that unhealthy, yet.

But what if you dwelled in your own drama? When you dwell in your drama you tell yourself how horrible it feels to be so fat and unhealthy, how uncomfortable your pants feel cutting into your gut, how sluggish and awful you feel being so out of shape, how sick and tired you are of launching those numbers on the scale, and how embarrassed you feel walking around looking so pudgy. Do you still feel like having that cupcake?

You shifted the threshold and deemed your current state as absolutely unacceptable. You have nowhere else to look but up. Now the fear (discomfort) of these consequences is more powerful than the pleasure of eating the cupcake; your focus is on avoiding *anything* that keeps you in this painful place.

Now when you have the thought, "It's not that bad" you will trigger a new when/then plan of action. You will leverage drama and reframe the bottom to where you stand right now. This skill can guide you in all those small moments of your day. It's your decisions in these small moments that become the difference between living well, or not, in achieving your goals, or not, in living effortlessly, or not.

---

**SMALL TASK:** *prove it. Write the statement, "It's not that bad" on a sticky note and put it on or near your computer. Notice when you say it and how often. What goal are you preventing yourself from having because of this paralyzing statement? Create a when/then action plan starting with, "When I catch myself saying, 'It's not that bad,' then I will immediately say, '_____,' instead." Notice how this shifts your motivation.*

---

## 25. LET IT MARINATE

IMAGINE COMBINING ALL THE TOOLS I've instructed you on in this book: use imagery to turn on your lighthouse and activate movement toward your end state, use your past challenges to create a strategic plan for the future, stay energized by shifting your motivators often, and reframe the bottom of your threshold to adjust and challenge your familiar zone. What would your life look like? What would you be able to achieve in a day, a week, a year?

Wait, there's more. I have one more strategy for you that will reinforce your process of being in a state of wisdom. It might even be the easiest and most enjoyable strategy, and yet so often overlooked: Celebration.

Have you ever heard the phrase, "You learn more from your failures than you do your successes?" Why do you think this is? When I pose this question to my clients, I hear some great and very true responses, such as: "It's because we learn the value of effort," "It makes us work harder next time," "We learn what we did wrong," "No one likes the feeling of losing." This perspective is so commonly accepted that it implies it's more important to fail than it is to succeed. To this, I disagree.

No doubt, failure and the ensuing discomfort knocks us out of our familiar zone, which we know well at this point. Failure gives us an incentive to avoid discomfort, and thus incentive to analyze our process. We look at what caused the failure and where the holes and leaks are our system that we can fix. It triggers us to apply effort, and associate effort with mastery, which fosters a growth mindset. What I disagree with is the perception that these insights can only be found in failure. In fact, you can learn just as much, if not more when you examine your successes.

We aren't deliberate with how we manage, analyze and celebrate success like we are with failure. Therefore, we don't gain the full value of the experience. If we treated success with the same level of attention and analysis as we do failure, then it can have an even greater impact because success offers one thing failure doesn't: An awareness of a state of achievement. You have the winning combination. All you need now is to reinforce that achievement by remembering your success, and accessing that memory in all its glory, again and again. When you enjoy the moment and relive the process, you are creating neural pathways for success and are more likely to succeed again. In fact, it becomes easier to succeed than it is to fail. This is huge!

This isn't just for the BIG achievements or wins. Again, think small and simple and in the moment.

For example, when I go to the gym, I used to take notice of the discomfort of my workout and breathe into it. I welcomed the discomfort and even enjoyed it because I associated this feeling with getting stronger. For a long time that was the primary focus of my workout; I would go to the gym and seek pain, then leave knowing I moved my threshold slightly.

I never paused to notice the feeling of achievement I felt after a workout. I never allowed myself a minute to sit and revel in the endorphins and positive shifts in my mind and body. By not paying attention and rushing off to my next to-do, these positive shifts didn't have a chance to fully integrate. The positive chemicals were quickly replaced with stress chemicals. This prevented my muscles from fully recovering, and my mind from comfortably shifting to a new activity. By skipping the opportunity to celebrate, I un-did some of the hard work I'd put into my workout. My achievement was diminished.

After many years of studying the science of performance and working with elite athletes, I began to understand the power of celebration and integrated this powerful perspective into my life.

One of the techniques I use I learned in yoga class. Every yoga practice ends in a pose called, sav asana (corpse pose). This pose entails lying on your back in a relaxed position with your eyes closed, and your mind free of thoughts. You are present and notice all the feel-good sensations you stimulated in your practice. Some people refer to this as nap time, but that's not the true intent. The true intent is recovery and integration. I now end all my workouts in this pose. When I finish my strength training, I stop, lie still on the floor of the gym, and allow my mind and body to fully absorb, integrate and celebrate the work I just did. I take full advantage of the opportunity to reinforce those success pathways.

Yes, there may be a few curious looks from other gym goers, but I simply smile because I know something they don't. This is the key to reinforcing success. I give you permission to do the same. Don't miss another opportunity. Don't leave the gym, the fitness room, Zumba, or spin class without absorbing the full benefits of that hard work. You deserve to celebrate!

When I say celebrate, I mean to simply be present in that moment and allow yourself to expand into those feelings and sensations that are components of that state. Note every detail, feeling, shift, sensation, etc. The more detailed you are, the more vivid it becomes in your mind, and the easier it will be to reactivate these neural pathways at will.

In other words, by practicing this often you soon will be able to ignite the success state, even before you've taken any action. Because I have practiced ending every workout lying on the floor in sav asana, and breathing into the feeling of accomplishment, I can activate that state as I start my workout. I can maintain this state of accomplishment and presence for my entire workout. And you know what else? I feel joy during my workouts. Previously, I only felt joy for a brief and fleeting moment as I rushed off to the shower. Now I can activate it and sustain it at will for long periods of time.

---

**SMALL TASK:** *celebrate and bask in achievement. Pick something you plan to accomplish today, complete the task, and then sit quietly with your eyes closed noticing as many details of your state of accomplishment. Treat it as if you were drawing a map for yourself, notice every sensation, feeling and shift. Breathe into it for two minutes.*

# Extraduction

The theme of this book is to seize small moments to reinforce an intentional state of being, called wisdom. If you take the time and make the effort to incorporate even some of the tools in this book you will be practicing wisdom. Your practice will result in many new avenues that further access this state of being. You will enhance your wisdom pathway and you will create a more energy efficient process. You will rewire your brain and body to prefer this state of being. This means if you maintain these micro-efforts, it will be harder to stray from wisdom than it will be to maintain it.

You may need to reread this book a few times before putting the strategies into practice. But keep in mind, we only remember 10% of what we read, and 90% of what we do. So, practice you must! Take your time incorporating each tool and add new ones as you feel ready or inspired. Revisit your processes often to see what works and what needs adjusting. Use your circle of influence to give you support and new insights. Continue seizing opportunities to learn, apply, and reflect.

Stay balanced and centered by noticing the cues from your body that tell you when you are off. Catch these cues and realign, recover, and energize before taking on anything new. This will maximize your ability to stay aware and open to each new moment and each new opportunity to practice being in a state of wisdom.

Start your day by turning on your lighthouse. Use your tools to reframe challenges to align with your purpose. Associate with those who have similar goals. Connect with people who enrich your life. Treat them well, give to them, and receive from them. Laugh and celebrate often. When you do this, you will live more and more in your bliss. Open yourself to notice and seize even more opportunities, and this will be your new normal.

Your wisdom pathways will soon be so highly grooved that you will operate from this state of wisdom without realizing it. It will be too hard and too uncomfortable to live any other way. If you stray even for a moment, you will easily bring yourself back to balance. You will feel joyful, peaceful, and limitless every day.
Congratulations. You are on the path to thriving!

# ABOUT THE AUTHOR

Meaghan K. Foley
Director of Performance Psychology
BrightDot

Meaghan has a master's degree in sport & performance psychology and is an NLP Master. She has a vast array of professional experience specializing in resilience, performance & mindset, strength & conditioning, imagery and neurolinguistic programming.

Meaghan is an authentic, charismatic presenter and teacher with over 10 years of coaching and training experience. Her clients range from beginning youth to elite professional athletes and come from all over the US: LA Galaxy Academy, Augusta Arsenal Soccer Club, Clairemont McKenna College, University of New Hampshire, just to name a few. She also trains executives and professionals from renowned organizations including Google, EXOS, Pierce Atwood and the US Military. Meaghan is an accomplished athlete and avid runner.

# BIBLIOGRAPHY

Anshel, Mark H. 2012. *Sport Psychology: From Theory to Practice*. Pearson Benjamin Cummings. San Francisco, CA.

Clement, Damien PhD, ATC, CC, AASP, Shannon, Vanessa R. PhD, CC, AASP, Connole, Ian J. 2012. Performance Enhancement Groups for Injured Athletes Part 2: Implementation and Facilitation. Sport Psychology & Counseling. *International Journal of Athletic Therapy & Training.* Vol 17 (5), pp 38-40.

Dobbin, A., Maxwell, M., Elton, R. 2009. A benchmarked feasibility study of self-hypnosis treatment for depression in primary care. *International Journal of Clinical and Experimental Hypnosis.* Vol 57 (3) pp 293-318.

Dweck, C. S. (2006). *Mindset: The new psychology of success*. New York: Random House.

Ellis, A. 1957. Rational psychotherapy and individual psychology. *Journal of Individual Psychology.* 13:38-44.

Ellis, A., and J.D. Ellis. 2011. *Rational emotive behavior therapy.* Washington, DC: American Psychological Association.

Ivey, Allen E, Ivey, Mary Bradford, Zalaquet, Carlos P. 2010. *Intentional Interviewing & Counseling, Facilitating Client Development in a Multicultural Society, 7th ed.* Brooks/Cole , Cengage Learning. Belmont, CA.

James, Matt. 2011. *Accelerated NLP Master Practioner Training.* Advanced Neuro Dynamics. Kialua-Kona, HI.

Jensen, M.P., Barber, J, Romano, J.M, Hanley, M.A, Raichle, K.A., Moulton, I.R., Engel, J.M., Osborne, T.L., Stoelb, B.L., Cardenas, D.D., Patterson, D.R. 2009. Effects of self-hypnosis training and EMG biofeeback relaxation training on chronic pain in persons with spinal cord injury. *Intentional Journal of Clinical and Experimental Hypnosis.* Vol 57 (3) pp 239-268.

Katiuscia, Sacco; Franco, Cauda; Federico, D'Agata: Davide, Mate; Sergio, Duca; Giuliano, Geminiani. 2009. Reorganization and enhanced functional connectivity of motor areas in repetitive ankle movements after training in loco-motor attention. Elsevier. Science Direct, Brain Research vol 1297, p 124-134.

McArdle, W.D., Katch, F.I., Katch, V.L. (2010). *Exercise Physiology.* Philadelphia, Wolters, Kluwer/Lippincott Williams & Wilkins.

McDuff, David R., Newsome, Ozzie. *Sports Psychiatry: Strategies for Life Balance & Peak Performance.* American Psychiatric Publishing. Arlington, VA.

Murray, John. F. 1998. *Emotional adjustment to sport injury: Effect of injury severity, social support, and athletic identity.* Retrieved April 20, 2009, from **http://www.smartproinsight.com/DissertationIntro.htm**

Nieman, DC, Exercise testing and Prescription: A health related approach, 4th ed., Mountain View, CA: Mayfield Publishing, 1999.

Ogden, Jane. 2007. *Health Psychology: a textbook.* McGraw-Hill House. New York, NY.

Pollock ML, Wilmore JH, Fox SM: Health and Fitness through Physical Activity. New York John Wiley & Sons, 1978.

Pool, Eva-Maria; Rehme, Anne K.; Fink, Gereon, R.; Eickhoff, Simon B; Grefkes, Christian. 2013. Network dynamics engaged in modulation of motor behavior in healthy subjects. Elsevier. NeuroImage vol 82, pg 68-76.

Roy, E. A., & Marteniuk, R. G. (1974). Mechanisms of control in motor performance: Closed-loop vs. motor programming control. Journal of Experimental Psychology, 103(5), 985–991.

Schmidt, Richard A; Wrisberg, Craig A. 2008. Motor Learning and Performance; a Situation-Based Approach. Human Kinetics. Champaign, IL. Pg 25-27.

Smith, Ronald E.; Ptacek, J.T.; Smoll, Frank L. 1992. *Sensation seeking, stress and adolescent injuries:   A test of stress-buffering, risk-taking and coping skills hypotheses.* Journal of Personality and Social Psychology. Vol 62, Iss 6, p. 1016

Walker, Natalie PhD, Thatcher, Joanne PhD, Lavalle, David PhD.2007. Psychological responses to injury in competitive sport: a critical review. *Journal of the Royal Society for the Promotion of Health.* Vol 127 (4) pp 174-180.